AMBER MASSIE-BLOMFIELD

Amber Massie-Blomfield is an arts producer and non-fiction writer. Her work has been commissioned and published by *Standart*, *Unbound*, *Annexe Magazine*, *The Wrong Quarterly*, *The Independent*, *The Guardian*, *Exeunt* and *New Internationalist*. She is a regular contributor to *The Stage*. She received the Society of Authors' Michael Meyer Award in 2016, and in 2018 a Special Achievement Award at the Off West End Awards for her work at Camden People's Theatre, where she was Executive Director from 2014 to 2018. She is a fellow of Birkbeck, University of London, and the Royal Society of the Arts. *Twenty Theatres to See Before You Die* is her first book. She lives in Brighton.

Twenty Theatres to See Before You Die

Amber Massie-Blomfield

Penned in the Margins

LONDON

PUBLISHED BY PENNED IN THE MARGINS
Toynbee Studios, 28 Commercial Street, London E1 6AB
www.pennedinthemargins.co.uk

First published 2018

Printed in the United Kingdom by TJ International

ISBN
978-1-908058-45-4

Image credits: Battersea Arts Centre: Edward Hands (Wikipedia); Camden People's Theatre: Edwan Munro (Flickr); Century Theatre: Andy Dingley (Wikipedia); Contact: Joel Chester Fildes; Grand Opera House: Ardfern (Wikipedia); Holbeck Underground Ballroom: Slung Low; Liverpool Everyman: Bs0u10e01 (Wikipedia); The Minack Theatre: Nilfanion (Wikipedia); Morecambe Winter Gardens Theatre: Nilfanion (Wikipedia); Mull Theatre: Colin (Wikipedia); National Theatre Wales: Grubb (Wikipedia); The Roman Theatre of Verulamium: Carole Raddato (Wikipedia); The Rose Playhouse: David Sim (Flickr); Rowena Cade: The Minack Theatre; Shelley Theatre: Shelley Theatre; Summerhall: Dogwoodfire (Wikipedia); Tara Theatre: Tara Arts; Theatre by the Lake: George Hodan; The Theatre of Small Convenience: Amber Massie-Blomfield; Theatre Royal Bath: Michael Maggs; Tom Thumb Theatre: The Thanetonian.

CONTENTS

For Ros, who loved the world.

There is something about empty theatres...
yes, they're full!

Here is Where We Meet

Twenty Theatres to See Before You Die

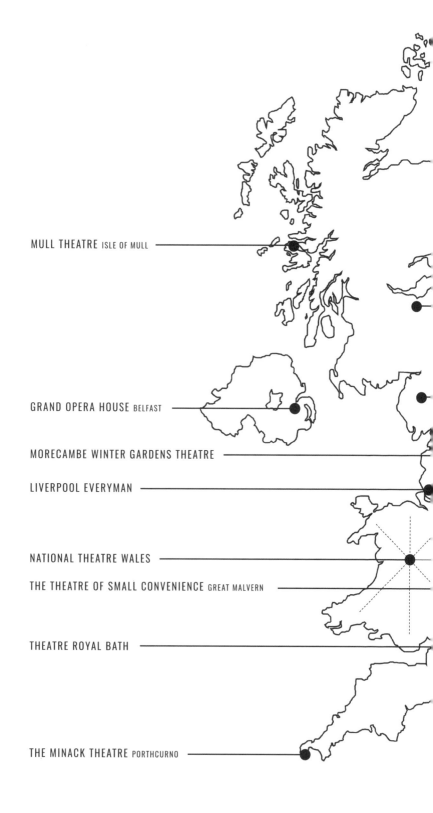

MULL THEATRE ISLE OF MULL

GRAND OPERA HOUSE BELFAST

MORECAMBE WINTER GARDENS THEATRE

LIVERPOOL EVERYMAN

NATIONAL THEATRE WALES

THE THEATRE OF SMALL CONVENIENCE GREAT MALVERN

THEATRE ROYAL BATH

THE MINACK THEATRE PORTHCURNO

Twenty Theatres to See Before You Die

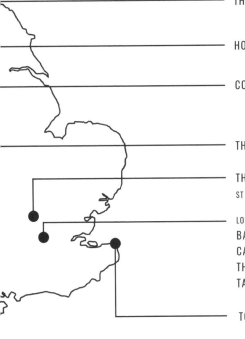

SUMMERHALL EDINBURGH

THEATRE BY THE LAKE KESWICK

HOLBECK UNDERGROUND BALLROOM LEEDS

CONTACT MANCHESTER

THE CENTURY THEATRE COALVILLE

THE ROMAN THEATRE OF VERULAMIUM
ST ALBANS

LONDON
BATTERSEA ARTS CENTRE
CAMDEN PEOPLE'S THEATRE
THE ROSE PLAYHOUSE
TARA THEATRE

TOM THUMB THEATRE MARGATE

SHELLEY THEATRE BOSCOMBE

INTRODUCTION

*Red velvet curtains. A chandelier. Golden plasterwork.
Tip-up seating. Followspots. The rain. Celtic carvings.
An earth floor. An eighties tower block. A country.
A cow byre. The smell of formaldehyde. The ghost of
Jack the Ripper. A bomb site. A sanctum. A Victorian
gentleman's toilet. Soot stains. A golden telephone box.
Four army surplus trailers.*

LET ME TELL YOU about this place.

The roof sprang leaks and the air conditioner broke down and the voices of passers-by disturbed the performances, penetrating the fire doors that opened directly from the stage to the street. In the foyer there was a beaten-up old piano no one could play, a wonky hatstand no one ever used and wobbly tables you couldn't set a drink on in confidence. Once, a ladies' community choir got trapped in the lift, moments before they were due on; the artistic director jimmied the door open and delivered them to the stage, breathless and giggling, just in time.

I was deeply in love. For all its shortcomings, this was a place of possibility. I watched Don Quijote stoke a revolution in makeshift cardboard armour here, and the minotaur reclaim their story as a glittery drag king cabaret. That it was rough around the edges was not, for me, incidental to its charm. It was, quite deliberately, set apart from the shiny façades of the surrounding high-rise office blocks and the exhausting commerce of central London. A clearing in the heart of the city.

The word for theatre comes from the Greek 'theáomai', meaning *to watch*. Or, better, *to behold*, which implies an exchange of sorts — as if theatre doesn't exist on the stage with the performers, but in the act of the audience taking possession of it. 'Theatre' is the word both for this movement of air and for the site where it happens. The art is live, indivisible from its place.

During the two years I had been working at Camden People's Theatre, the truth of this had become apparent. No matter the care a director might give to the tilt of an actor's face or the timbre of a line, an audience's experience of the evening's entertainment was as much framed by how easily they had found the theatre, how comfortable the seats were, their memory of what had happened here before, or the stories they had heard about this oddball corner of Euston. The fabric of the theatre contained something distinctive: whatever happened could only happen right here. And if this was the case of our venue, I thought, wasn't every theatre crowded with its own influencing forces — each with a unique story to tell? As John Berger said of empty theatres: *yes, they are full.*

In 2016, I began plotting an adventure. It was the wake of the United Kingdom's vote to leave the European Union, and in the fractious atmosphere of that summer I found myself thinking not only about the stories of Britain's theatres but also their purpose. 'Theatre is the most complacent place in the world,' one friend had written on Facebook, despondently, in the days following the referendum. The issue, it was true, had barely broken the surface of the nation's stages. Still, I could not be dissuaded of the idea that there was something that theatres — only theatres — could offer us now. You can take any empty space and call it a bare stage, but it seemed to me extraordinary that up and down the country there are so many places designated for this purpose, citadels to self-expression, to big ideas and imagination and the electrifying power of people getting together in real time, in a real place to think about what it means to be human. But how, I wondered, do so many continue to thrive, despite the ongoing threat from funding cuts, reduced education in the arts, and a culture of instant online gratification?

There was only one way to be certain. I had to get on the road and find out for myself. What I had in mind was a freewheeling trip around Britain's most remarkable — and unusual — theatres. I wanted to get off the beaten track, finding the venues with a story worth the telling: theatres in unique settings and with fascinating histories; theatres that have thrived in unlikely circumstances or where people have, in one way or another, reimagined what a theatre might be.

I started planning my route by writing to 100 friends and colleagues with a simple question: what is your favourite theatre in this country? The responses proved revealing. In the emails, tweets and letters I received in the weeks that followed, certain venues appeared time and again: Cornwall's Minack; The Tom Thumb Theatre in Margate; The Watermill, Newbury; Mull Theatre and Keswick's Theatre by the Lake —

a catalogue defined by distinctive settings and which represents some of the best-loved playhouses in the country.

Many people suggested the places where they had hung out in their youth. For Theodore Bass it was the Playbox Theatre in Warwick. Eleanor Turney nominated Theatre Peckham and David Lockwood the Playhouse in Cheltenham. Matt Trueman wished to take me to 'Greeker' at Bradfield College — a replica Greek theatre carved from a disused chalk pit in the grounds of the school he had attended. They could not have meant so much to those of us who hadn't snuck crafty fags in the fire escape or participated in 'the Michaelmas Term tradition of Handshaking'. But no matter: these were first-love theatres and the passions they inspired were private and unconditional.

I took delight in discovering theatres I had never heard of before. The Shelley Theatre in Boscombe, for instance, which Danielle Rose told me was 'built by a family of writers and activists', or The Ashcroft in Fareham. 'It's a converted school with an ancient plane tree which grows up, over, and under the building,' wrote Hannah Ashwell in her email to me. 'The bricks of the building are covered in engraved initials. We've been an arts centre since Dame Peggy Ashcroft opened the building in 1989, but it's much older than that.'

I received nominations for performance spaces that are not theatres at all. 'A random village hall in Devon,' suggested

David Lockwood. Laura Barnett proposed the recently formed National Theatre of Wales, which has made a virtue of being itinerant, creating a roving programme of Welsh productions that consider the entire nation their potential stage. Kate Cross suggested a roaming theatre in a caravan. Chris Goode suggested a theatre in the palm of his hand. These contrary nominations pointed to an uncomfortable truth that I would have to tackle: the deep associations theatres carry in their brickwork are not always entirely positive, and sometimes it is necessary to step outside in order to be free of them.

Theatres that are no longer there or are on the cusp of disappearing. The subterranean vaults of the Arches in Glasgow. The Broadway in Peterborough, which Rosie Curtis told me I must visit 'before it is turned into luxury flats' — a common refrain. Chester's Roman amphitheatre, now little more than a stretch of parkland. I mourned, with Andy Field, 'the delirious and utopian space that the Shunt Vaults once occupied in London Bridge — an impossible place behind a tiny hidden door from which many other spaces stole so much superficially whilst ignoring that it was not the exposed brickwork that made it special.' That impossible place where we stayed up until dawn on Easter Sunday, where a bouncer found my boyfriend passed out in a tuk-tuk, and where I once mistook someone receiving a blowjob for performance art. We could never go back.

I realised that what I had in my possession was a kind of 'anti-canon' of theatres. Was I approaching, already, some fundamental truth about what defines a great theatre? As with the playhouse in the Victorian gentlemen's public toilet, often it was its eccentricities that made a theatre special, rather than the plushness of its décor or the starriness of its line-up. Certainly it affirmed my impulse to be led, not by any attempt at a comprehensive overview of British theatres, but by my own curiosity.

Camden People's Theatre even received a generous nomination, from Olly Hawes. 'When I walk in, it always feels like I'm taking another step as part of some sort of crusade — here is a building that heroically supports the type of work I believe in,' he wrote. Sometimes heroism really is as modest as sticking your hand down the back of a broken toilet, over and over again. Or is that insanity?

I put up a map on the drawing board above my desk and pinned little flags of torn white paper to it. Achieving a good geographical spread, I thought, was important. It would be easy to write only about theatres in London, but making the entire trip on my Oyster card would not have made for much of an adventure. I limited myself to four, sacrificing venues like Theatre Royal Stratford East and Shakespeare's Globe after much deliberation, and eschewing the theatres of the West

End which, for all their beguiling glitter, would have felt at odds with the spirit of the nominations I'd received. I adopted three principles: firstly, the theatre should be in a building or location that was in some way unusual; secondly, that it must host public performances (albeit, in some instances, sporadically); and, thirdly, its story must speak to my sense of what theatres can mean to their communities.

Porthcurno to the Isle of Mull: a dot-to-dot journey across the country in a battered Morris Minor, alone and fancy-free. It didn't happen like that of course. Mostly, I crammed in my trips around running the theatre, sneaking off at weekends or claiming time off *in lieu*. One Friday evening, on a stuffy coach somewhere in the Midlands, as I gazed out at neat, semi-detached houses where someone had put a paddling pool out on a lawn, where school children strolled home licking ice lollies, their chins turning sticky in the sun, I questioned the ill-considered impulse that meant I was here, rather than sitting in a beer garden with my mates. But I was too far in. The only way out was through.

As I travelled around, the recommendations kept coming, and my list of theatres shifted. I received urgent tip-offs and pursued a breathless trail through Google. How could I have so nearly let this one slip through the net? Each recommendation was a gift, presented with care. Over a breakfast of salty bacon and eggs in a Keswick B&B, a dining room full of walkers insisted I write down the names of the theatres they loved: Frank Matcham's Grand Opera House, Belfast; The Bush in west London; The Oldham Coliseum — everyone jostling to explain why their nominee was more deserving of being on the list than any other. A man at Caerleon Amphitheatre in Wales was adamant, when I spoke to him on the phone, that I shouldn't visit — 'It wasn't a theatre, really, they mainly killed animals here' — but told me about Verulamium, home to the oldest visible remains of a theatre in the country, and the next day I was on a train to St Albans. During a break in rehearsals, theatre-maker Caroline Horton casually mentioned an old 'theatre on wheels' that travelled around Britain in the 1950s, bringing performance to remote communities still reeling from the aftershock of war. It was a fantastical image, something out of post-apocalyptic literature. Only months later, while researching Theatre by the Lake in Keswick, did I join the dots. Soon afterwards I found myself in an abandoned industrial park in Leicestershire, performing the can-can to an empty auditorium.

There were so many theatres I couldn't fit in. I couldn't find purchase on the story of the much-loved Watermill Theatre in Berkshire, so I let it go. I became briefly obsessed with Plas Newydd in Anglesey, the country pile of Henry Cyril Paget, the 'dancing marquis' who converted his chapel into an ornate, 150-seater theatre and brought scandal to Victorian society with his lavish lifestyle and extravagant theatrics. But through several telephone calls to the National Trust, I was persuaded that there was nothing to see — his successors had demolished the theatre.

What you hold in your hands, then, is the collection of theatres I arrived at through this slipshod approach. While I couldn't include all of the nominations, I hope the theatres I have chosen reflect the spirit of them. Undoubtedly, you will have your own views on the theatres I've included here: which I should have left out, which ones I've missed. Good. Start your own list. Have your own adventure. As much as this book is a love letter to the theatres contained in its pages, it is a celebration of all Britain's theatres. The Theatres Trust estimates there are over 1,300 of them.

I've arranged the chapters in an order that makes sense to me. Although *Twenty Theatres to See Before You Die* is not a comprehensive history, early on I've included five venues — the Roman Theatre at Verulamium in St Albans, The Rose Playhouse in Southwark, Theatre Royal Bath, the Grand Opera House, Belfast, and Liverpool's Everyman — that offer snapshots of distinctive periods in the development of British theatres.

Exploring my personal history with theatre leads me on to Battersea Arts Centre, where I found my footing after moving to London aged 19. The fire that destroyed its Grand Hall in 2014 prompts wider reflection on the connections between theatres and the memories they contain.

Theatres, I began to discover, are often haunted places. I took a rather literal approach to exploring this notion when I joined an all-night ghost hunt in Morecambe's abandoned Winter Gardens. The themes of loss and mutability also resonate in my exploration of the theatre built by the son of Percy Bysshe and Mary Shelley in Boscombe, Dorset.

The macabre setting of an old anatomy lecture hall in Edinburgh proves that theatres need not always be in venues specifically designed for the purpose. And if a theatre can be anywhere, why not in a disused Victorian gentlemen's toilet — as in the case of Malvern's Theatre of Small Convenience?

In chapters on Mull Theatre, Tara Theatre and Contact, I reflect on the bonds that form between theatres and the specific communities they serve. I then visit Slung Low's Holbeck Underground Ballroom in Leeds, Century Theatre, Theatre by the Lake, Margate's diminutive Tom Thumb Theatre and National Theatre Wales — each one an example of how people have, in one way or another, radically rethought what a theatre can be.

Finally, inevitably, I return to my own shambolic, lovely Camden People's Theatre, animated by a renewed belief in the importance of sustaining these buildings. Even, perhaps especially, those theatres where the roof leaks and the lift breaks down. Where nothing seems to work but anything is possible.

But first, on the south-west tip of Great Britain: a story that epitomises the unwavering love for theatre that has motivated so many of the characters contained herein; indeed, the same love that motivates me.

An implausible tower. Seaspray. Barbed wire. Sorcery. An upturned wheelbarrow. Loved ones lost at sea.

1

THE MINACK THEATRE

Porthcurno, Cornwall

An implausible tower. Seaspray. Barbed wire. Sorcery.
An upturned wheelbarrow. Loved ones lost at sea.

ON THE BEACH AT ST IVES, a man is building implausible towers. He chooses the largest stones, great grey seals scattered across the shore that have been weathered smooth by time and motion, bending his knees beneath the heft of them. Then — with a pace that's either meditative or agonising depending on your disposition — he balances the stones on top of each other, moving with his breath to find the smallest contact point, a hair's width from tipping.

I join the audience that has gathered on the promenade. Together we watch him, momentarily captivated by his feat. We murmur into little ripples of applause after each balancing act. Some purchase postcards from his wife at a stand nearby. The towers begin their unlikely ascent to the sky.

We have long been infatuated with towers; the spectacle of them, the reminder of how far our grasp might stretch. A tower is a symbol of perseverance and defiance, a human disruption to the natural order. In *White Sands*, Geoff Dyer writes about the Nuestro Pueblo Towers: 17 strange, rocket-like structures that climb up to 30 metres into the skyline above Watts, Los Angeles. Crafted from cement, wire and a menagerie of found objects — broken bottles, porcelain, tiles, seashells — they were created by Sabato Rodia, an Italian construction worker who laboured alone over 33 years to bring this magnificent folly of his own invention into being.

'His purpose,' Dyer writes, 'was perhaps similar to that

of people who climb mountains. Maybe the only answer to the question of why Rodia built his monument is a negative version of Hillary's famous response about why he had climbed Everest: because it wasn't there.'

I am thinking about Rodia's towers the next day. Standing at the furthest tip of Cornwall, I gaze from the cliff down at a sprawling structure that appears to have been hewn from the rock. The Minack looks like something out of time, an open-air theatre from a forgotten race, so unlikely on this remote outcrop of south west Britain that it must be the product of an alien culture. An avalanche of terraced seating falls away down a steep gully, sporadic outbuildings tipping slate rooves forward as if at any moment they might tumble over and come crashing down on the sharp ridges of granite that jut into the Atlantic below. Haphazard paths and precarious stairways snake across the steep terrain, bending themselves to the contours of the land. Great lichen-dappled boulders shrug up through the earth. The auditorium is pockmarked with splashes of colour, violent oranges and pinks, tropical flowers and succulents clinging tight to the cliff.

 The stage, far below, is a wide, odd-shaped strip of stone, scattered with columns and archways, a raised round dais and a sweeping stairway befitting grand entrances. Beyond it, I can make out a strand of bleached sand along the coast; the ocean, cyan spilling into ink; and the sky, bright and clear today. A summer holiday sky. It's the kind of view people come to gaze at and to post on Instagram. The theatre could easily be upstaged by this landscape, but in fact, in their unlikely union, the theatre and its surroundings amplify each another. Later, I will become obsessed with the theatre's webcam, returning often to take in the landscape, glitchy and low res through the rain-splattered lens, on smeeching winter mornings with the sea fizzing and angry, or at night, when all I can make out is the faint outline of granite, an electric glaze of moon on water. In the early 1930s, Rowena Cade stood here, perhaps on this very spot, looked out at a scrubby, inhospitable patch of cliff, and imagined a theatre. How she realised her remarkable vision through decades of arduous labour and sheer bloody-mindedness is, for me, one of the most inspiring stories of holding faith in theatre.

Rowena was born in Derbyshire in 1893 and spent much of her childhood in Cheltenham before moving to Cornwall with her mother in the 1920s. While living in rented accommodation in Lamorna, six miles up the coast, she came across the Minack headland overlooking Porthcurno beach and bought it for £100. The pair built a house on the site and moved in soon after.

Rowena joined the local amateur dramatics group, and in 1929 she designed and made costumes for an open-air production of *A Midsummer Night's Dream*, to be performed in meadows nearby — all gauzy fairy wings and lopsided pixies' hats. The Great Depression was bringing its blunt fist down on the nation, a black and white newsprint collage of grim-faced men with flat caps and placards, tired children in worn clothing. It must have seemed a long way from Rowena's idyllic Cornish outpost, her days spent swimming in the sea, conjuring Oberon and Titania in countryside 'quite over-canopied with luscious woodbine, with sweet musk-roses and eglantine'.

But her life had been touched by the turbulent history of the early 20th century. The First World War brought an end to a genteel upbringing. She found herself in a job breaking horses for the army in Elsenham and living in an old shepherd's caravan. Her two brothers went away to fight; the younger never fully recovered from the mental impact of 'shellshock'.

In 1917, her father died of natural causes, and after the war, her mother sold their home in Cheltenham. She and Rowena set off on the road, spending a nomadic couple of years travelling the country, trying to find purchase in an unsettled world. They came to rest here in western Cornwall, a place that still feels remote, far removed from the traffic of human life. In 1931, *The Tempest* was proposed as the next show to be staged by the local amateur dramatics group. It's easy to see why these cliffs overlooking the Atlantic so readily suggested themselves as a setting for Shakespeare's tale of turbulent storms, shipwrecks and loved ones lost at sea.

That winter, with the help of her gardener, Billy Rawlings, Rowena set to work. Together they blasted the site and used the granite they extracted to craft the first, green-cuticled terraces of seating, the grassy patch of stage. Rowena would harvest sand from Porthcurno beach below the site and climbing the headland, goat-like, with the sack of sand slung over her narrow back. She mixed the sand into cement, forged it into stairs and rows of hard seating, carved with Celtic designs of her own invention. Slowly, through a momentous effort of physical labour, the wild gully began to resolve into a theatre, ready for its first audience on 16th August 1932.

The theatre was Rowena's life's work. For more than half a century she kept at it, spending harsh Cornish winters hauling timber and ballast up from the beach, working tirelessly, late into the evenings, often alone. It was an epic undertaking and her tools were no more sophisticated than a wheelbarrow, a hammer and chisel. She would make improvements ready for the next summer's shows, adding a throne for *Anthony and Cleopatra* or a new dressing room. The seating rake began to spread outwards and upwards, sightlines determined not by design but by the contours of the landscape. Eventually the auditorium was capable of holding up to 750 people. She carved the names of the plays performed here into the rows of seating as she built them. *The Lion in Winter*. *Under Milk Wood*. *The Government Inspector*.

Shortly before she died, Rowena built a new structure: a balcony for a production of *Romeo and Juliet*. It juts into the playing space — an inconvenience, obscuring the audience's view of a key upstage entrance — but it is maintained now for posterity, a part of the iconic geography of the Minack's stage.

The balcony reveals a tension present in many places of performance. A building is typically designed for posterity, intended to outlast the players and audiences that currently inhabit it. But plays are always tumbling to their own ending. The briefest and most vivacious of artforms, theatre derives its energy from how much it is an object of the present.

Rowena had a more profound grasp of the symbiosis of these elements than most theatre architects. The notion that any part of her creation might become sacred would, I think, have seemed absurd to her. She was forever blowing bits up — sticking gunpowder underneath a seating box that dissatisfied her, knocking down the stage backdrop and rebuilding it. She would rather re-craft the space than constrain the play to the structures of the theatre.

"The theatre, for her, was like building sandcastles," declares architect Simon Crosse in *The Minack Theatre, Past and*

Present, a documentary about the history of the theatre. For, like sandcastles, the Minack's beauty was in part a function of how soon it might give way to the turn of the tide. The theatre was evolving, animated by change. So she kept working.

Do people do things like this anymore? Do they hold a single vision alight for an entire lifetime, pursue it so doggedly to the exclusion of all else? I think of what it must have taken on those excoriating mornings to drag yourself out of bed, bones cracking, and face the whipping winds and the icy sea spray; to haul bags of sand up that sheer cliff again and again in pursuit of a dream that could so easily seem frivolous, quixotic.

When the Second World War came, Porthcurno, which was the site of an important cable office, was considered vulnerable to attack and fortified accordingly. The Minack was commandeered as a lookout. Prisoners of war were brought in to clear the site. A gun turret went up, pillboxes were built and a ring of barbed wire installed. By 1945 the War had laid waste to Rowena's theatre. Stone by stone, she rebuilt it. For her, there was no other option.

The Minack is big business now, number one on TripAdvisor's list of Cornish tourist attractions, and a fine example of the economically generative value of theatres, if you're given to couching such things in terms that chancellors understand.

Each year, around 120,000 playgoers take their seats in the steep ranks that Rowena crafted.

I come back for the evening's performance, arriving early to take in the last of the sun before the show starts. I pull into the makeshift car park in a field on the edge of the site and join the gaggle of people making their way towards the theatre. They are weighed down with cushions, stacks of blankets, picnic baskets and ice coolers. We emerge at the clifftop, gaze down over the steep bank of seats. In the fading light, strings of bright globes illuminate the pathways. There's a festival atmosphere: people settling into their places, forming nests with their blankets and cushions, sharing sweets with neighbours, eliciting the loan of a bottle opener. Prosecco corks are popped. The heady combination of booze, glass, concrete and height is thrillingly at odds with health and safety imperatives. A teenager wanders around in a thick fleece dressing gown, a pair of binoculars on a string around his neck. There are many North Face jackets.

It is easy to mythologise what happened here. Rowena was able to do what she did because she came from an affluent family; she had the personal wealth to pursue what others would consider a folly. Unlike Rodia, her labour didn't happen at the end of a tough day's work in the quarries, an adjunct to the irksome business of having to earn her bread and butter. This was the substance of her life, and being able to make a project like this the substance of your life is a privilege.

But it took all she had. By the end of her life, she was living alone with her six Cavalier King Charles spaniels in just one room of Minack House, cooking herself sparse meals, going without heat in the winter. She struggled to keep things going, twice unsuccessfully inviting other organisations in to help run the theatre. It was long after she died in 1983 that the Minack Theatre began to thrive as a business. Still, she kept faith with her creation to the last, sustaining it with her own diminishing funds, making minor additions and necessary improvements.

Rowena possessed a singularity of vision usually permitted only to men. How often she had been described as eccentric, even mad. But the men in Rowena's family, like so many men, were gone, and perhaps in times like this, when the social anchors that have held society in place are set loose by the raging tides of war, dedicating your life to that which you truly believe in, letting that be what steers you, is the pragmatic thing to do. Still, as television presenter Judi Spiers says in *The Minack Theatre, Past and Present*, "I don't think there's any other theatre you can point to and say: do you know, a woman actually laid those blocks, pulled the beams up for the dressing room."

I have caught the last of the day's light. The evening is coming in fast, and it's cloudy, but there's a thin band of pale pink through the sky, and we watch it fade through mauve, aubergine, until all the sky is royal blue, and the moon is a pale plate behind scattered clouds.

The production is *The Crucible*, performed by a predominantly amateur ensemble. The Minack has always been a stage for amateur groups — some companies have been coming here since the 1960s and '70s, from all over the country. Rowena was herself an amateur with no formal training in architecture or theatre, and the presentation of non-professional work here is a tradition tied to those summers of the 1920s and '30s, when there was so little for the local community to do in their leisure time that they made their own entertainment. How fine it must have been to spend the summer with friends, out in the open air, sinking into Shakespeare's seductive, insistent poetry. How magical to greet your audience in this secret jewel of a theatre, to witness their delight as they crest the clifftop, and then, as it darkens, to bring forth Prospero, Caliban and Ariel, lit only by car headlights and the par-can moon. The midnight matinees of the 1950s. The nights when the rain came down in stair-rods and the cry went up from the auditorium: "you play, we stay!"

Besides, there's always the stage-flat sky and the sea, the impromptu choruses of distant porpoises, bit parts for basking sharks. Olly says he 'spent the entire time looking at the horizon. Over the course of the play a tanker moved achingly slowly from left to right. It was amazing.' Rowena's theatre invites attention not only to the drama of the plays, but also to the drama of nature. It is a reminder that nature is its own spectacle, worthy of our contemplation.

Tonight, the enormity of the backdrop lends itself brilliantly to Miller's tale of sorcery and the supernatural. The Atlantic is a plain that stretches over 3,000 miles, uninterrupted, from here to Salem, Massachusetts. As the night deepens, the actors light a great fire pit at the centre of the stage. Flames flash against the black sky. It's impossible not to be bewitched.

I have a photograph pinned above my desk at home. A rusting, salt-spotted wheelbarrow has been upended; it forms an impromptu chair. Rowena is sitting in it. She is reading a book, her concentration undivided, a shock of white hair blustering about her, crazed by the weather. Her skin is tanned and deeply marked with wrinkles. She wears leggings, grey knee-high socks trimmed with burgundy, black slippers and a thick herringbone knit. Granite boulders rise in a bank behind her, disappearing out of shot. She looks entirely at ease, lost in her own world.

What are you reading, Rowena Cade? I'd like to be able to climb into the frame, to gaze over your shoulder. But the words are forever lost, unknowable.

No matter. The picture speaks of action. In a moment she must spring to her feet, seize up her tools and continue her work: to build a place where words and ideas become manifest. Taking time to find a chair would be a waste. A wheelbarrow does just fine.

That was Rowena Cade. All propulsion, forward trajectory; a restless creature in constant pursuit of her wonderful, confounding dream: a symphony in stone.

She built it because it wasn't there.

2

THE ROMAN THEATRE OF VERULAMIUM

St Albans, Hertfordshire

Boudica. Black ash. A litter of rubble. A violin.
Tweed plus fours. A dropped Maltesers wrapper.

I AM WANDERING FROM ST ALBANS STATION along the quiet meander of the River Ver, through Verulamium Park. On this pristine April day, there are signs of life everywhere: blossom and flickering sticklebacks in the water and moorhens fucking. Lifted on the air, from a distance: the shouts of children. Two teenage girls in school uniform are having an extravagant argument about a dropped Maltesers wrapper. The wrapper is blustering dangerously close to the river's edge.

Misshapen grey chunks of Roman wall breach the surface of the parkland at odd intervals, tracing a clumsy, dot-to-dot outline of an ancient city. This wall has stood here for nearly two millennia, through the coming and going of centuries, a silent witness to the giving way of generations. Its resilience pays tribute to the craftsmanship of the anonymous hands that laid the stones — as far as walls go, this one is exemplary.

The adventure I'm setting out on is all about stones — the stories they contain and the voices with which they speak. I'm here to see the oldest ruins of a theatre that can be visited anywhere in Britain, and one of only a few Roman theatres known to have existed in this island.[1] By tracing the physical

---

[1] More popular at the time were the gory delights of the amphitheatre, distinguished by its circular or oval shape, where animal baiting, gladiatorial fights and military displays took place. Remains of these can be seen in locations such as Caerleon and Chester.

origins of Britain's theatre history to this spot, I hope that I might discover why sites like this matter and why, in spite of all the innovations and distractions that the millennia have thrown at us, we keep coming back to theatres.

Outside the Six Bells, I fall into conversation with an elderly chap in a hat with unseasonable earflaps. He points out the spot behind the pub where, in 2012, the team filming *Rory McGrath's Pub Dig* for Channel Five excavated a Roman hotel. Now it's covered in tarmac, a patio full of empty garden furniture awaiting the bustling trade of the first sunny Friday of the year.

History is thick beneath our feet. Verulamium was the name of the third largest city in Roman Britain, situated in the southwest of what is now St Albans, Hertfordshire. It remains mostly unexcavated, locked in beneath the park, private farmland and neighbouring buildings. Turning the earth, archaeologists found a layer of black ash: evidence of the revolt led by Boudica in around 61AD, when this Roman stronghold was burnt to the ground and several thousand people killed. But Boudica's rebellion was defeated and in around 140AD, as Verulamium burgeoned once again, a theatre was erected.

On the outskirts of town, situated on a low hill between two fields, it is a bowl in the earth roofed with sky, open on one side where the stage would have been. The ground is scarred with lines of grey brickwork. Two concentric walls covered with moss delineate the outer perimeters of the *cavea*, where the audience sat, the exterior marking where the theatre was expanded in around 300AD. Grass pathways lead down to where gates would have been, giving entrance to the arena. Nearby are the sketched outlines of the dressing room and a row of shops: the bronze worker's, the carpenter's and the wine shop.

A single pillar rises nearly six metres from the stage. It is a reconstruction that offers a sense of the scale of the playing space. The original is likely to have formed part of a rustic attempt at a *scaenae frons*: the permanent, ornate backdrop that stood behind the stage in most Roman theatres. At Verulamium, audiences may have witnessed the popular Latin and Greek plays of the period or the 'pantomime', mime performances with dancing and music. Bullfights and sword fights probably took place here too, in the broad, gravel-covered arena at the foot of the basin. The space where the stage once was is now a view of field where, beneath the earth, the remains of a temple lie. A red tractor rusts, undisturbed, and a herd of sheep champs the grass peacefully.

'A stadium in repose is a bowl of latent noise, suspended emotion: unheard chanting, the ineradicable cheers of phantom crowds. Like the scummy afterglow left in a drained coffee cup,' writes Ian Sinclair in *London Overground*. He was talking about Millwall Football Club's ground in south east London, but it stands for places like this too, places of gathering — you feel the ghostly mark on them. You hear echoes.

The theatre at Verulamium could hold around 2,000 spectators. Imagining it, I think about how alien the encounter might be if, by some strange knot in time, we were to find ourselves alongside each other. Which would prove more frightening to the other, their reality of blazing cities and gladiator fights or mine of genetic modification and cat memes? And then it strikes me that perhaps we would try to find common ground, and in so doing we would tell each other stories. We would be travellers, new to one another's countries, conveying tales of war and art and family and love, and it would be this exchange that formed a bridge between us.

Today, the site is mostly empty. A dad is explaining things to his uninterested young son. An energetic, silver-haired couple is taking a selfie.

'In a simple direct sense, archaeology is a science that must be lived, must be "seasoned with humanity." Dead archaeology is the driest dust that blows.' So said Sir Mortimer Wheeler, the extravagantly moustachioed archaeologist and

Keeper of the Museum of London who directed the first, partial excavations at Verulamium in the early 1930s.

Rather than a kind of mnemonic for what once was, to be viewed through plates of glass and from behind rope partitions, Wheeler recognised that it is the conversation between the past and present that gives history its value. His project was to animate the past, taking advantage of the burgeoning media landscape of his own time to bring the significance of historic sites to a broader constituency.

One story from the Second World War, when Wheeler was stationed with Field Marshall Montgomery in North Africa, seems to characterise the man perfectly. Soon after Britain had secured control of Libya, he was dismayed to see soldiers vandalising Roman ruins and so, like a prototype Indiana Jones with a cut-glass accent, he took a leave of absence and headed off across the country in a Jeep to significant historical locations such as Leptis Magna and Sabratha, claiming a 'highly exaggerated authority' to harass senior officers into posting guards, erecting 'out of bounds' signs and lecturing troops on the importance of the sites. His actions are credited with saving many historical artefacts. Later, he starred in a string of TV programmes like *Animal, Vegetable, Mineral?* and *Buried Treasure*, bringing his field to life with warmth and humour.

Before he had become a household name, Wheeler,

together with his wife, Tessa Verney Wheeler (a prominent female archaeologist in her own right at a time when prominent female archaeologists were a rarity), led the excavation at Verulamium between 1930-34. They were joined by a cohort of volunteers and students earning their salt by spending a summer with the Wheelers.

As Rowena Cade began work on her theatre in west Cornwall, here the parting soils revealed burial sites, intricate mosaics and, of course, a theatre. Wheeler ensured that Pathé films were on hand to capture it all. It wasn't only this wealth of mud-clogged treasure that made the site one of the hottest archaeological hangouts; the Wheelers and their team were also developing new excavation techniques such as the grid-based Wheeler-Kenyon method, still in use today.

Curiously, histories of British theatre have mostly ignored the structure they disinterred here. Perhaps this is too much of an anomaly to be accommodated. Traced backwards, the line runs adrift with mummers' plays and the mystery cycles in the murky waters of the Middle Ages. This only serves to make the theatre at Verulamium all the more remarkable; an isolated enclave, sending out semaphore across time.

Len Scammell. 1924-1997. He lives doubly who also enjoys the past.

I sit down on a bench on the edge of the site and survey the ruins. Then, attempting to make sense of my view, I look up other, better preserved Roman theatres around the world on my phone. I gaze at images of Merida in Spain; even on my tiny screen it seems vast, two floors of Corinthian pillars behind a large stage, marble bright in the sun.

Theatre had been thriving in the Roman Empire for around 500 years by the time it made its way to Verulamium. Theatre buildings had evolved over the centuries from temporary wooden structures designed for festivals to sophisticated stone edifices capable of holding thousands. Vitruvius set out the model for the Roman theatre in his authoritative work on architecture, *De Architectura*, written at the end of the 1st century BC. He gave specific instructions about everything from the location of theatres, which should be as 'healthy as possible' — avoiding the possibility of winds from 'marshy districts and other unwholesome quarters' — to the necessity of including bronze vessels in niches between the seating, an ingenious early amplification system designed to enrich the clarity and resonance of the actor's voice. There is an appealing simplicity to his method for planning the layout of the theatre itself. 'Having fixed upon the principal centre, draw a line of circumference equivalent to what is to be the perimeter at the bottom, and in it inscribe four equilateral triangles, at equal distances apart and touching the boundary line of the circle, as the astrologers do in a figure of the twelve signs of the zodiac, when they are making computations from the musical harmony of the stars. Taking that one of these triangles whose side is nearest to the scaena, let the front of the scaena be determined by the line where that side cuts off a segment of the circle (A-B), and draw, through the centre, a parallel line (C-D) set off from that position, to separate the platform of the stage from the space of the orchestra.' While his directions were followed with varying degrees of fidelity (most theatres, including Verulamium, seem to be loose riffs on this model), the elegance of Vitruvius' approach has stood the test of time.

I scroll through images of other theatres — Orange in France, Amman in Jordan. Then I stumble on a YouTube clip from the Roman theatre at Palmyra, Syria, a UNESCO world heritage site that has become the unlikely staging ground for a propaganda battle at the heart of this decade's grimmest theatre of war. In the video, a concert is taking place. Blinking against the desert light, clad all in black with white baseball caps to protect them from the sun, musicians from Russia's Mariinsky Theatre Orchestra are seated in the midst of the majestic ruins of the theatre, surrounded by intricately carved stone pediments and Corinthian columns. A violin strikes up Bach's 'Chaconne'. The notes soar into the sky.

The concert was held in Palmyra in May 2016 by the

Russian Government to celebrate the role of the country's military in the city's liberation and to commemorate the victims of the war. The orchestra was assembled in the spot where, just 10 months before, ISIS fighters had lined up 25 captives and executed them by shooting them through the head.

The ruins of the theatre at Palmyra had become a symbol, co-opted by the Russians to declare their commitment to liberty and freedom of expression. It was a counter to the propaganda war waged by ISIS through bloody videos on YouTube and Twitter, dignifying a country that had in the last few years become synonymous with body bags and razed cities. The image of musicians playing in this charged setting, within earshot of the artillery bombardment from the frontline, is captivating. It also belies Russia's own human rights record.

Watching the concert on my phone screen, I think about what historic cultural sites can come to signify to societies at times of crisis. The camera pauses on a photo at the back of the stage, framed in black — a man with neatly clipped white hair and glasses, reading at a lectern. Khaled al-Assad, the head of antiquities in Palmyra, was murdered by ISIS in 2015. Having assisted with the evacuation of the city museum, al-Assad was captured and tortured for one month. He refused to reveal where the artefacts were hidden, so he was executed, his body displayed in a public square.

ISIS recaptured Palmyra in December 2016. In January they planted explosives at the theatre, destroying the *scaenae frons*. Now, where the Russian orchestra played, a litter of rubble lies underfoot. For anyone who has ever wondered if theatres really matter, we might seek an answer by asking why someone might seek to destroy one. Theatres are places of the corporeal — you show up in the flesh, you put your body where your mouth is. Theatre can be an expression of defiance.

This period of Roman theatre history was brought to an end by authoritarian paranoia about what dangers the theatre might let loose. In the 4th century, Rome adopted Christianity as its state religion; theatres became associated with pagan ritual and were therefore maligned. In 526, Emperor Justinian ordered theatres to be closed altogether. The theatre became the town's rubbish dump, accruing a sea of refuse that filled the arena, spilling across the stage and the auditorium. That was fine by the archaeologists; you can learn a lot about people from their rubbish.

Few performances are staged at the Roman Theatre of Verulamium today, but in July a local amateur company takes it over to present an open-air show among the ruins. When the day finally arrives, I don't want to go. I'm knackered. It's been pouring with rain all afternoon and I don't want my new haircut to go frizzy.

But I go. I pull on my cagoule and my wellies and travel to St Albans under skies that look like a sample pallet for a Farrow and Ball paint range. I join the queue of locals streaming into the site. It seems I'm the only person here who doesn't know everyone else. People conduct voluble conversations over each other's heads, becoming louder and louder, everyone talking at once. "I've just read *Jude the Obscure*, have you read that? It's the worst book ever written. I mean, it's very good, but I'm going to read *Macbeth* to cheer myself up," hollers one man to his friend at the other end of the line. It's still chucking it down. At a trestle table I buy a pint of local Three Brewers real ale and then negotiate my way down to the ruins over slippery grass, struggling to hold my beer aloft.

In the auditorium, a man in galoshes wipes down a plastic chair for me with a sopping towel, making it even wetter. The point will come soon where everything here is as saturated as it possibly can be. The atmosphere will attain a kind of equilibrium where we no longer have to worry about anything being any soggier than anything else, and we can all relax and enjoy ourselves. After all, in spite of our protestations to the contrary, British people rather like it when it rains. We don't feel entirely ourselves if we don't smell vaguely of wet dog. And what could be more wonderful than watching a play called *A Midsummer Night's Dream* in the middle of a deluge? "It would have been so nice to be able to wear a summer dress," sighs a woman behind me, delighted.

Tonight's show is sold out — it has been for weeks — and seeing the auditorium full of people like this makes it seem much bigger than during my last visit. I think back to the quiet patter of the dad who stood here then, pointing at things and trying to engage his son with the joys of history, the long shadows they cast on the gravel. It might have been a different place. This disjuncture with the Verulamium of my memory is heightened by the fact that the stage has been set up at the opposite end to where it would originally have been. It wears against the grain of the place — unsettling, somehow, to turn your back on the spectral players of the past; but the sense is fleeting. I take my seat and cloak myself against the damp with a deep draught of ale.

The set is what I can only describe as a deep-sea-acid-rave-Celtic fortress, and the play, when it begins, is the most off-the-wall thing I've ever seen on stage. A new metastructure has been added to the play-within-a-play, locating it in a school classroom. There's a mystifying subplot about a fall-out over who went on the best summer holiday, which gets unceremoniously ditched without resolution around the interval. When Helena and Hermia fall out, they do a duet of Taylor Swift's 'Bad Blood', and Snug the Joiner gives a magnificent rendition of Katy Perry's 'Roar as the Lion'.

It's all utterly wonderful: silly, unglamorous and unlikely

to change the world — yet I doubt I could have had a better time at the RSC or Shakespeare's Globe than being one of this crowd, up on our feet in the rain, whooping and clapping and joining in with the chorus of 'Superstition', beaming up proudly at family and friends — who are, for me, strangers. This night, I think, has precisely its own weight, is just what it needs to be, belonging to these people, this place. And it strikes me in the end that us being here, the simple generosity with which this show has been created, and the open-heartedness with which it is met, binds not only the audience and the performers, but those that stood here two millennia ago, and those who might stand here two millennia hence. We keep showing up. Even in the deluge, when it would be so much easier not to, we keep showing up.

As the night deepens, the stage lights catch the rain falling across the exposed stone ruins. They glitter in the dark.

3

THE ROSE PLAYHOUSE

London

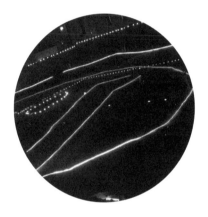

Plastic flowers in a hoarding. Hot soup. Orange diggers. Hell's mouth. Judi Dench's feet.

IN MAY 1989 A PROTEST was taking place on London's Bankside.

Hundreds of people had gathered, banners aloft: *Please don't Doze the Rose*; *We're a Thorn in their Site*. Someone had woven a row of plastic flowers into a hoarding. A man with an electric piano struck up a song: *It will be lovely! It will be great! Perhaps the past will reincarnate! When the Rose Theatre blooms again...*

Among the crowd were familiar faces — Dustin Hoffman, Alan Rickman, Vanessa Redgrave — youthful in 1980s knitwear and stonewash jeans. The RSC company had popped down from the Barbican to give an impromptu performance of *Henry VI*. One protestor reported spotting Rosemary Harris, star of the *Spiderman* movie franchise, serving tea and sticky buns from a trolley. The atmosphere was somewhere between a vigil and a street party, the air electric with the energy that accretes in places where people gather. The protestors clustered around a huge hole in the earth, perhaps two storeys deep, the footprint of an office block where, in the dirt, a team of archaeologists were carrying out their intricate labour.

The unprepossessing brickwork this glittery line-up had turned out to protect represents one of the most significant heritage sites in theatre history anywhere in the world. Built in 1587, the Rose was one of the earliest purpose-built theatres in London. It was here Christopher Marlowe staged his early plays and here that *Titus Andronicus*, Shakespeare's gloriously bloody tragedy, received its premiere. The foundations of the theatre had been exposed during work to build a new office block on the site. Planning permission had been granted on the basis that the developers would fund an archaeological excavation before construction began.

One of London's great Elizabethan playhouses had been uncovered for the first time, and its condition was better than anyone had hoped. As the archaeologists dug, the earth began to give up fragments that had been buried for centuries, together enriching the historical understanding of theatre-going at the tail end of the 16th century. But on the evening of Sunday 14th May 1989, only hours before construction was due to commence, the fate of what remained of the playhouse was hanging in the balance. Nearby, a chorus of orange diggers was waiting, vulture-like; soon they must make their way onto the plot to prepare it for the foundations of the modern office block and all chance of preserving the Rose would be lost.

A maddening Saturday afternoon in the middle of a July heatwave and I'm sweatily elbowing my way from London Bridge station through the hoards in Borough Market. The market celebrated its thousandth birthday in 2014 — rewind a millennium and perhaps I might have run into King Canute sipping a flat white from Monmouth Coffee or Edward the

Confessor queuing for a chorizo burger. In spite of the huge changes the market has gone through in its transition from grocery wholesaler to foodie hotspot, I have always felt there is some irreducible spirit of the city here, in the noise of it, the dogged but warm-spirited bartering, punters plonking themselves down anywhere, on window ledges or the edges of dirty pavements, unwrapping overspilling packages of meat grilled in the mucky London air. Outside the Market Porter pub, a crowd of drinkers is standing in the sun, clutching pints, idly people-watching. That's just about one of the happiest places you could be.

It was here in Southwark, on the south bank of the Thames, where, more than a thousand years after Verulamium's life as a working theatre came to an end, playhouses began to thrive once again: The Globe, The Swan, The Hope and The Rose. The area was known, evocatively, as the Liberty of the Clink. Being, as it was, outside the jurisdiction of the City of London, it became a place where bearbaiting, brothels and outdoor theatres, proscribed in the City, were permissible — in short, all the things that constituted a bloody good day out at the turn of the 17th century.

I turn out of the market along Park Street and the hubbub of the crowd quickly fades behind me. I wander past a modest gated estate called Old Theatre Court — the original site of the Globe Theatre, now recreated in precise detail a couple of hundred metres up the road on Bankside. Shakespeare's Globe, as the reconstruction is called, is one of my favourite theatres, and if I'm ever at risk of feeling disenchanted with the artform I return to it. There is nothing better than an evening spent surrounded by that raucous crowd, who respond to the fights, music and excessive crotch thrusting as if they were at a music festival. A reminder of the popular collective experience this can be — and how far removed it is from the conservative offering of many of London's major theatres. But it's a simulacrum; the remains of the original lie here, beneath paving stones. I gaze through the black railings — the site is marked with little more decorous than a small bronze plaque, a couple of information boards and some pot plants.

I'm not here to visit Shakespeare's Globe today. Instead, I want to uncover the narrative of a playhouse that has quite literally been buried, a site that not only provides a link to a pivotal period in theatre history, but also illustrates the passion theatres inspire in the communities that surround them.

It's easy to get lost looking for The Rose Playhouse. You might expect it to be something of a landmark, a venue packed with tourists and doing a stiff trade in keyrings and souvenir dismembered body parts. Instead, it's blink-and-you'll-miss-it. A single black door tucked in a corner beneath Southwark Bridge marks the entrance; a blue plaque and a sandwich board indicates the way in. What remains of the theatre is hidden inside the basement of a vast, shimmering, eleven-storey building: home to the Crown Prosecution Service.

Inside it is cool and quiet, a world away from the bustle of Bankside. It takes my eyes a few moments to acclimatise after the bright sunshine outside. The theatre consists of a small, dimly lit and odd-shaped wooden platform, ringed on three sides by shallow banks of seating and display boards telling the history of the site. A vague smell of damp hangs in the air as in so many of London's fringe theatres. Then, beyond the stage, the floor falls away into a swell of darkness, a void that presses up beneath a ceiling of metal girders; stripped bones braced beneath the weight of the office building above. The site is covered by a dull expanse of water, with odd banks and islets of rough concrete breaking the surface here and there. A weird, Ballardian landscape.

A narrow plank juts out over the pool. Strands of red lights like flares or fireworks beneath the surface trace the alignment of the structures that stood here in Marlowe's time: a timber frame with a thatch roof, open to the heavens, two 14-sided, three-storey polygons within one another — the larger 22 metres in diameter, the smaller, 14 metres across. An arcing line indicates the edge of the space where the 'groundlings' would have stood — the joyous bunch of noisy, standing spectators who paid a penny to enter the theatre and have a jolly good time heckling and 'pippin pelting' the actors.

I first learnt about the Rose Playhouse from my school drama teacher — an ageing Irish hippy with a scrubby beard and John Lennon specs — in one of his characteristic rants about Margaret Thatcher. It was 2000, and the site had only reopened to the public the previous year. For him, what had happened here was a symbol of the worst excesses of the neo-liberal politics of the 1980s; how the imperatives of capital were allowed to run roughshod over both the arts and Britain's cultural heritage.

I was immediately fascinated. The uneasy accommodation between heritage and commercial interests that was ultimately reached — with the playhouse remains preserved *in situ* in the basement of the office block — spoke to my growing sense of the position theatre has long held in relation to the state; somehow necessary, but also with the potential to be unsteadying. Not to be given too much air.

Philip Henslowe, the original proprietor of the Rose, may well have recognised this characterisation. He was a man who operated in the fringes of civilised London society. In addition to being a theatre owner, he also ran the Paris Gardens, an animal-baiting venue. He was the landlord of numerous properties, including inns and brothels, and a moneylender. A figure occupied with activities both desired by the City and reviled by it.

In 1587, Henslowe went into partnership with John

Cholmley, 'citizen and grocer', to build one of London's first permanent theatres, following the Red Lion in Whitechapel (1567), The Theatre in Shoreditch (1576), Newington Butts in modern-day Elephant and Castle (1576), and The Curtain in Shoreditch (1577). The layout of these new buildings had much in common with the animal-baiting yards where strolling players had become accustomed to performing. Standard features included galleries, a yard, a 'tiring house' (or dressing room) and 'my lord's room' — designated for the nobleman whose patronage was required for the company to operate.

The Rose thrived and in 1592 the playhouse was expanded to cater for demand. Henslowe logged the day-to-day transactions of the theatre in meticulous detail in his diary, which still survives in the archive at Dulwich College. It offers a fascinating insight into what life at the playhouse must have been like, with its records of box office takings, advances paid to playwrights and loans made to actors. His inventory lists props including 'Hell's Mouth, a tomb of Dido, trees, mossy banks, and a wooden canopy'. The diary even includes a collection of spells, designed to help retrieve a stolen object or deal with a dog bite.

In *The Illusion of Power: Political Theater in the English Renaissance*, Stephen Orgel writes, 'Before this moment, the concept of theatre had included no sense of place. A theatre was not a building, it was a group of actors and an audience; the theatre was any place they chose to perform ... [Once] embodied in architecture ... theatre was an institution, a property, a corporation ... For the first time in more than a thousand years ... an established and visible part of society.' The construction of the Rose, and other institutions, re-established in the public psyche the synonymy of the two meanings of theatre — the building and the activity that takes place within it.

What remains of the Rose is protected, hidden under a thin case of concrete beneath the water's surface. There's nothing to see here, really. A reflective plain that invites an act of imagination. To see it half submerged, bereft of its purpose, lends it a sense of melancholy. I find it difficult to imagine, as I stand alone, how it must have been in the days of Henslowe, with hundreds of people packed into this modest site. Difficult to imagine how Marlowe's *Doctor Faustus* (with the eponymous hero played by the legendary actor Edward Alleyn) must have struck an audience for whom appearances of the diabolical seemed a genuine possibility. Anecdotes from the time report that the incantations in the play had inadvertently caused an actual occult apparition, with 'one devil too many' appearing on the stage. (If not a reflection of the power of Marlowe's writing, it is certainly testament to the talents of whoever was doing the play's publicity.)

As they delved into the earth, the archaeologists uncovered artefacts that reveal the human stories behind the theatre. A manicure pin. A shoe with a hole sliced in it to relieve a bunion. A gold ring with the words *Think of me, God willing* engraved on it in French — the story of the giver and the wearer now lost, but the hope it represents undiminished. They even discovered indentations where rain had dripped from the thatch protecting those in the more expensive gallery seats.

Performances at the Rose took place in broad daylight, the audience's presence acknowledged and celebrated by the performers on stage. Ian McKellen wrote about the intimacy of the Rose in the *Daily Mail* at the time of the protest, the way the audience 'could catch every smile and frown, every blink of the eye ... the poetry and rhetoric could be spoken with a conversational tone: they could even have whispered, and not a syllable be lost'.

Perhaps it was this haunting sense of proximity that moved the protestors on that Sunday evening in 1989. Judi Dench reported to a journalist that a few days before, she had taken off her shoes and stood in the spot where the stage had been, as if through contact with the ground she might come closer to the past; a symbolic earthing.

As dusk fell, the fate of the theatre was still uncertain. The crowd had grown to around 3,000, all anxious to hear the news that it would be preserved (and perhaps to catch a glimpse of someone they knew from the telly). At midnight, the site would legally be returned into the hands of the developers, Imry Merchant, to begin construction. The builders were due at 6 a.m. the following morning.

Simon Hughes, then MP for Southwark and Bermondsey, spoke to the assembled crowd. Asking who would be willing to stay all night, around half raised their hands.

"We will remain through the night and into the morning, to act as guardians of the Rose until they come and tell us that they are willing to act as guardians too," he said. "They are accountable to a wider community, and we represent that community now ... we will not be moved."

They kept their vigil all night. Some attempted to sleep, lying down for a few hours of fitful rest. Others stayed awake, drinking hot cups of soup provided by volunteers, clouding the cold air with their breath as conversations about the site's fortunes continued. When day came, the diggers arrived. But as urgent meetings between the developers, MPs and English Heritage took place, work was suspended. By the afternoon the protestors received word that the Government had agreed to a deal with the developers; they would pay £1 million to delay the build and find a workable solution that would allow the remains of the playhouse to be preserved.

The protests brought about some unanticipated victories. In 1990, PPG 16 was introduced, following the debates prompted by the campaign in Parliament. This new legislation governed how the impact on historically significant sites of new building developments must be mitigated. 'Archaeological remains are irreplaceable,' it states. 'They are evidence of the past development of our civilisation ... They are part of our sense of national identity and are valuable both for their own sake and for their role in education, leisure and tourism.' This led to the preservation of an entirely different theatre of the period, The Curtain in Shoreditch, home to the Lord Chamberlain's men. Its remnants were uncovered in 2012 during the construction of a 40-storey residential block; plans are now in place to develop it into 'a captivating tourist attraction ... featuring the preserved remains of The Curtain Theatre and a purpose-built heritage centre, visitors will also be able to take a break at the sunken amphitheatre or even watch a performance.'

While the campaign stayed Imry Merchant's hand, the Rose site was not, as many of the protesters wished, purchased from the developers by the Government and turned into a heritage destination with a roof, museum and gift shop. Instead, the plans for the building on top of it were amended. The foundations of the theatre were preserved, covered in a membrane, sand and ballast, then flooded with water to prevent cracking. Here they remain, buried in a state of suspended animation, awaiting — what? Much like the preservation of the Roman Theatre at Verulamium, this is an act of faith for future generations.

But what would a satisfactory future for the Rose Playhouse look like? In the lobby, there is an architectural model box showing what the Trust envisages; not a museum — or not only a museum — but what looks like a pretty fine, modern, high tech theatre. An £8 million transformation will, it claims, introduce a clean, contemporary stage and seating bank, a floor with glass panels revealing the architecture of the ruins underneath. It suggests a hat tip to history, a quiet conversation with it, rather than an attitude of deference. The Rose, as Simon Hughes has said, is 'not intended to be a museum. It's intended to be a living, breathing space'.

It is possibly sentimental to believe it matters that performance continues to happen here. After all, London has plenty of arts venues. What we lack is the resource and societal infrastructure to fill them with invigorated, inspired artists and audiences ready to address the issues that are relevant right now. In this context, the energies expended on a heritage campaign might seem misplaced. A more fitting tribute to Shakespeare and Marlowe's legacy would be the insurance of a thriving future for the artform — of brilliant *new* art and artists.

I notice someone has scribbled a sign and left it lying by the pool: *Here lies one whose name was writ in water.* The poet John Keats' epitaph, engraved on his tombstone at his behest instead of his name. His words are a reminder that, at its heart life is transient; one thing always giving way to another.

But it's a disingenuous binary, as these things so often are; a society that values its creative heritage is more likely to appreciate the arts today. A positive sum game in which contemporary culture is enriched by exploring and understanding the past.

I return that evening to watch *Titus Andronicus.* "This is the first time *Titus* has ever been staged again in the place where it had its world premiere in the 1590s. Don't you think that's remarkable?" one of the volunteers asks me, and I nod. Then she adds, ruminatively, "Well, there was a production a few years ago, but it wasn't very good, so I don't count that one."

It is a suitably gory production by a young, international company. The action is expansive, ranging across the playing space, now awash with lurid green and blue light. Passages are performed down on the ruins themselves and then on the wooden stage a few feet in front of us. As I sit in the darkness, watching the action unfold a few feet from me, I recall McKellen's words about the motivations behind the campaign to save the Rose.

'It is more than an actors' shrine: it is a symbol for everyone. It is a symbol of our need to communicate. It was built before we depended on the telephone and the television ... The Spirit of the Rose celebrates person talking to person, directly, one with another; and looking each other straight in the eye.'

4

THEATRE ROYAL BATH

Somerset

*A fire. Jane Austen. Lost summer afternoons. Five
white male playwrights. Bohemia. A rabbit. A royal
coat of arms. My God and My Right.*

1992. TWO SISTERS WERE BAKING a cake, and it was going horribly wrong. They began with the best of intentions, but now there had been a misunderstanding about an instruction to "beat it", and things had descended into mayhem. One sister launched into a misguided juggling routine with half a dozen eggs that crunched wetly on the floor; the other made a joke about some "big jugs" of water that seemed cryptically adult. Soon, they were embroiled in a food fight, the air thick with spilt flour, custard poured over lurid barnets, faces planted in bowls of cake mixture. The auditorium of the Theatre Royal Bath was uproarious with laughter. But I was stony faced and on the edge of tears. Turning to my Mum, I said, "You wouldn't like it, would you?"

The pantomime that Christmas was *Cinderella*, featuring an unlikely line up of *Birds of a Feather* star Lesley Joseph, former England rugby player Gareth Chilcott and a pre-Operation Yewtree Rolf Harris as Buttons. I remember how upset I was. The mayhem on stage, the cross-dressing, the mess and the fighting — these were not a laughing matter. I had a metallic taste in my mouth. The theatre seemed a place where forbidden things were not only possible, but celebrated. Where the world was turned on its head. My mum was certain it was a sign that I hated theatre. She was wrong.

If the Roman Theatre at Verulamium is the starting point of British theatre history, that evening in 1992 was where the history of my own relationship with theatre began — at the Theatre Royal Bath. What am I hoping to find by returning? Perhaps I'm seeking a connection with whatever it was that first seduced me in the theatre. Could some of the thrill of that night in 1992 still be contained in the brickwork? What would it take to unlock it?

Arriving now, the theatre seems smaller than I remember — it's been quarter of a century, after all. I approach from the bottom of Westgate Street. Tonight, the creamy Bath stone façade of the building is uplit against the royal blue sky. Three sets of double doors are thrown wide open to the street. Above the entrance, twelve large windows are arranged over two floors, all ablaze with lights, and the Royal coat of arms, several feet high, 'New Theatre Royal' engraved in stone over the top. *DIEU ET MON DROIT.*

All around me, people are disembarking from taxis, chattering excitedly. It's clear they've made an effort. There are suits and velvet skirts and well-coiffed hair. Inside, drink orders are discussed and programmes purchased. Two men compare notes on what they know about tonight's show, *The Winter's Tale*: "It's strange, but that's Shakespeare's fault, not the company's". Black and white production shots from past shows line the walls: *Private Lives, The Dresser, Measure for Measure*. We gaze up, wondering from which TV dramas we recognise the actors.

I pause on the threshold of the auditorium. 900 seats face the stage, slowly filling up. The ritual of tickets checked at the door, the fuss over coats, the ungainly shuffle past patrons who have already taken their places. Everything seems to lean forwards, arranging itself for what is to come. A meeting of worlds.

The Theatre Royal Bath is a wedding cake, gaudy and fabulous, gold-touched plasterwork ascending in three sugary tiers, curving in a lyre around the stalls. Rich burgundy house tabs are raised on a sparse set, at odds with the ornate grandeur. High overhead, a vast chandelier forms an inverse fountain ablaze with a thousand splinters of light.[1] This is the theatre of public imagination, the image conjured in a thousand thespian clichés. In his book *In Place of A Show*, Augusto Corrieri writes of 'the *théâtre à l'italienne*, or 'the theatre we have in mind', as the historian Fabrizio Cruciani names it: a *forma mentis*, a structure imprinted on the mind, capable of conjuring, as though out of thin air, red curtains, balconies, plush seats, wings, orchestra pit, etc.' All a bit much, this confection of velvet and glitter; the vertiginous ceiling; the smell of burnt dust that's stayed too long in the dark.

---

[1] I have long been curious about how they clean this chandelier. It turns out they have a pulley system.

The plays I have seen on this stage come back to me, now, in freeze frames. A giant shows huge, iridescent, bubbling bottles of 'dreams' to a tiny puppet Sophie in *The BFG*. Macduff's son is seized naked and slippery from his bath in the RSC's *Macbeth*. A man, all in white, steps into the spotlight with a real rabbit in his arms — the opening of Complicité's *Light*, which I came to watch three times in the week it was here, learning the sparse, elegant language of the stage, the way that a branch can stand for a forest. I was falling in love.

In my teens, I would pay £3 for a standing-room-only ticket and then, when the lights went down, sneak into one of the best seats in the house. I remember the red velvet itch on the back of bare legs on the summer afternoons I spent at matinee shows while my friends were smoking spliffs in the park. At fifteen, I was at odds with the world, a slightly chubby teen with pink streaked hair and a Barbie T-shirt several sizes too small — trying to hide my insecurities beneath an unconvincing display of fearlessness and thick kohl eyeliner.

In a confusing world, theatre was something steadying. Here — gazing up at the bright lights on stage, or cramped into dark spaces, whispering with my youth theatre friends in the wings — everything seemed to find its order. In a diary from the time, I wrote of my joy in realising that, no matter what, theatre would be a place that would always welcome me — as a performer or an usher or an audience member, it would be somewhere to return. I was at home in the held breath at the end of the play, the pause after the lights go down and before the applause begins.

After each play had finished, I would go around to the back of the building, look up at the façade where another drama was playing out. From where I was I could see the actors in their dressing rooms, unaware they were being watched, standing in front of the huge Georgian floor-to-ceiling windows, wiping away greasepaint, removing wigs and shrugging off costumes. They belonged to another world, but a world that seemed tantalisingly close.

It wasn't just the plays that beguiled me. The Theatre Royal Bath is one of the finest examples of Georgian theatre architecture in the country. It opened at its current location in 1805, when Bath was in its prime — a period encapsulated in the writing of the city's unofficial patron saint, Jane Austen, who lived here between 1801 and 1806.

In her novels *Northanger Abbey* and *Persuasion*, Austen conveyed something of the breathless excitement of the city, the extravagant nights out at the Pump Rooms and the Assembly Rooms, the heady mix of fashion, wealth and gossip. Bath was a youthful city, full of potential, a place where things happened. The Theatre Royal Bath, which Austen visited at its original site in Orchard Street, was one of the bustling hubs of the society she documented. And, as is suggested by the bright lighting that was favoured in the auditorium throughout the performances of the time — a night at the theatre was as much about audience members watching one another as the performers on stage. Catherine Morland, heroine of *Northanger Abbey*, spends an evening at the theatre preoccupied with the question of whether her love interest Henry Tilney — who she fears she has offended — will look in her direction. That he remains engaged in the action of the play and doesn't spend the evening exchanging glances from his box opposite is read by her as a slight.

Many of today's theatre-goers would be horrified by audiences' behaviour at the time — the Georgians were noisy and liberal in their consumption of food and alcohol, even, on occasion, pelting actors with rotten fruit and vegetables if their performance was deemed unsatisfactory. They were not compunctious about making their feelings on proceedings felt; indeed, in 1809, performances at the Theatre Royal Covent Garden were disrupted for three months by rioters objecting to increased ticket prices, in the so-called Old Price Riots.

The theatre moved to its current site from Orchard Street, where it had thrived throughout the 18th century and had, in 1768, been awarded a royal patent, making it the first provincial Theatre Royal in the country. George Dance the Younger, one of the foremost architects of the era and professor of architecture at the Royal Academy, designed the new building. Dance created a striking, broad Neoclassical frontage on Beaufort Square, six pilasters running up the front and topped by grimacing theatrical masks carved into the stone.

But in 1862, a fire almost entirely destroyed the building. Around some of the windows, the pale stone still has a pinkish hue, discoloured by the heat of the blaze. An article in *The Times* on 24th April documented what happened:

'The flames burst through the windows with terrific fury ... so rapid were the flames and intense the heat that everything within the theatre, even to the iron pillars that supported the tiers of boxes and gallery, were consumed and melted in less than two hours, and the place was a bare ruin.'

A grainy photograph from the time attests to the devastation: a litter of broken beams and scorched brickwork, cavernous doorways a storey up opening to nothing. The space is filled, uncannily, with daylight, flooding in from where the roof should be; seven men stand unsmiling in the ruins, eyes shaded by oversized top hats. The theatre was vacant when the fire took place, so fortunately no one was hurt.

What was lost in the flames? In *The Empty Space*, the pioneering theatre director Peter Brook writes, 'I can take any empty space and call it a bare stage. A man walks across this empty space whilst someone else is watching him, and this is all that is needed for an act of theatre to be engaged.'

But no space, with a man walking across it, is empty. It becomes a place, and a place is more than bricks and mortar; it is memory, and history, and politics, and all the other psychological resonances brought by those that move in it. For better or worse, an act of theatre cannot be divorced from the network of associations accumulated in the location in which it occurs.

A fire. Jane Austen. Lost summer afternoons. Five white male playwrights. Bohemia. A rabbit. A royal coat of arms. My God and My Right.

I think, too, that what happens is not only that a place influences the activity that occurs within it, but that the activity begins to mould the place around it. The simple fact is that an empty theatre isn't empty at all. The seats angled expectantly towards the stage, the lights tilted on anticipated action, the props ordered on tables to be grabbed between scenes, banks of costumes ready to be shuffled on and off with haste: all these things may be understood only in relation to the human activity that has been, or is to come. They speak of presence.

'A place is more than an area,' writes John Berger in *The Shape of a Pocket*. 'A place surrounds something. A place is the extension of a presence or the consequence of an action. A place is the opposite of empty space. A place is where an event is taking place.'

The Theatre Royal Bath was rebuilt remarkably quickly, with the new building opening in March 1863. Architect C.J. Phipps moved the frontage of the theatre to Saw Close, into the former home of Richard 'Beau' Nash and his mistress Juliana Popjoy. Nash, the famous dandy, was Bath's Master of Ceremonies in the 18th century and synonymous with a certain calibre of bourgeois decadence.[2]

The theatre reopened with a production of *A Midsummer Night's Dream* starring a teenaged Ellen Terry, who would go on to be considered the greatest Shakespearean actress of her generation. Over the years that followed, the theatre went through mixed fortunes, until it was purchased in 1979 by a trust led by Jeremy Fry. He oversaw an extensive programme of renovations, enabling the stage to receive touring productions from major national companies, and is widely credited as the 'saviour' of the theatre. Now the theatre is a thriving regional hub, a major success story in economic terms — reflecting an affluent local population and a bustling tourist industry. The venue has a reputation for reviving classic plays, many

---

[2] It is alleged that Juliana was so distraught when Beau died that she spent the final 30 years of her life living in a hollow tree.

of which go on to lucrative runs in London's West End. It is a picture at odds with the prevailing narrative of half-empty regional theatres struggling to make ends meet.

Tonight, a mixed crowd is here to watch Cheek by Jowl's new adaptation of *The Winter's Tale* before it heads to the Barbican Centre in London. I fall into easy conversation with the man sitting next to me. Like me, he is attending alone. He speaks with a thick West Country accent that makes me feel instantly at home. Theatre, he explains, has only become part of his life recently — as a working class black man growing up in Bristol, it wasn't somewhere he felt particularly welcomed. But over the last few years he has discovered a passion for theatre and has been travelling all over the region to watch shows. Indeed, he has been 'bitten by the bug' so much that he's been inspired to give it a go himself; he'll be mounting, and starring in, a one-man adaptation of an Edgar Allan Poe story in the spring.

The lights are about to go down, so we perform the rituals of the theatre-goer: triple-checking our phones are switched off; tucking away our drinks so they won't get kicked over; shuffling in our chairs to find a comfortable spot. I send up the small, silent prayer of the audience member. *Please, let it be good.*

Occasionally, for a little while, I stop watching the play, and I pay attention to the audience instead. I listen to the special quiet in a theatre, which isn't really silence at all, but a muted John Cage soundscape of breath, tiny shifts of numb bums in seats, valiantly stifled coughs. Our quiet is something distinct from the silence of being alone. It's a reminder that presence isn't necessarily the same as self-projection. Chris Goode again: 'Really watching, and really listening, is not not-doing-anything. They're big things to do.' In the noisy world we inhabit, they feel like a gift.

Later, there will be applause, a spilling-out into the night, the play carried on into debates in bars, conversations in taxi cabs, suddenly remembered, and understood afresh, in a shower tomorrow, a dinner party next week, maybe even years hence; when grief comes, or love — this play in some small way having equipped us to face the present.

Later, the working lights will come up, revealing the scuffed stage, spotted with gaffer tape, and in the gantry overhead, rows of cooling, ticking lanterns. The get-out will begin and through the night, as we are sleeping, Bohemia and Sicily will be dismantled, packed up in trucks and shipped out, heading east on the M4 towards Oxford and next week's audience.

But for now, we are here, together on the play's brink.

Everything is possible.

5

GRAND OPERA HOUSE

Belfast

Mercury. A gold elephant's head. Seven gas burners. The Gods. A balaclava.

THE LOBBY OF THE EUROPA HOTEL is full of teenagers. Tonight is prom night and they're all dressed up to the nines, girls in jewelled frocks tripping about in too-high heels, boys with acne and frosted tips in badly fitting tuxes. "Come into my arms!" one girl hollers to her friend across the lobby, before flinging herself at her, laughing. "Sorry about all the noise," the receptionist shouts to me as I check in, over the sound of squealing.

This exuberant scene belies the Europa's reputation as 'the most bombed hotel in Europe'. Between 1970 and 1993, this central Belfast hotel – a popular haunt of journalists - suffered bomb damage over 30 times during the period of 'the Troubles'. From my bedroom window, I have a view of a car park, and beyond it an illuminated wall. The wall bears an image of William of Orange and the date — 12th July 1690 — when this hero of the Protestant community, dubbed 'King Billy', defeated the forces of the deposed Catholic King James II in the Battle of the Boyne. In 2012 this mural replaced a more contentious adornment. *YOU ARE NOW ENTERING LOYALIST SANDY ROW / HEARTLAND OF SOUTH BELFAST / ULSTER-FREEDOM FIGHTERS.* The image showed a balaclava-clad paramilitary fighter holding an AK47, alongside two red hands of Ulster, clenched and raised.

In Belfast, murals are synonymous with the Troubles; hundreds still appear in working-class communities of all stripes. They were both an artistic expression of political belief and a means of marking territory. The change here was a sign of more peaceful times in Northern Ireland that were ushered in at the end of the 1990s by the Good Friday Agreement. Today, in Belfast, the murals have become an unlikely tourist attraction; you can even take a 'taxi tour' to visit them or follow the GPS references in *The Belfast Mural Guide*.

The Grand Opera House is next door to my hotel. It's a red-brick edifice occupying the prominent corner plot where Great Victoria Street meets Glengall Street and surrounded by grey, angular new-builds. Frothing cream scrolls ascend to two onion-domed minarets, which frame the building's original name: *CIRQUE AND GRAND OPERA HOUSE*. Bold lettering promises *ARTS, MUSIC, DRAMA*; looking closer I see fine stained-glass windows, a jester leering from the stone. Above the entrance, extending from the crush bar on the first floor, is a room made almost entirely of glass; it has the appearance of an elevated conservatory or greenhouse. High above the junction, a gold-leafed figure of Mercury glows intermittently in the beams from passing traffic. He stands on one leg, arm raised skywards, messenger of the gods, ready to take off.

This is Frank Matcham's theatre. Matcham is a name synonymous with great theatres: the Grand Theatre, Blackpool;

the Hackney Empire; Buxton Opera House; London's Coliseum; Edinburgh's Festival Theatre; the Gaiety Theatre on the Isle of Man... the list goes on and on. He is considered the most prolific — and by many the greatest — theatre architect of all time. He designed at least 80 new theatres across the country, as well as being involved with the redevelopment of many existing buildings. As I seek to understand what makes a great theatre, I want to look closer at what was so special about the venues he crafted. His work is a cornerstone in the built theatre environment; and yet his approach was very different to today's architects.

Opened in 1895, the Grand Opera House is considered by the Theatres Trust to be 'probably the best surviving example in the UK of the Oriental style applied to theatre architecture': a building celebrated for its opulence, and also its sense of humour. It is remarkable, too, for everything it has withstood over the years. Flooding in 1901; a fire in 1934. Repertory performances took place here throughout the Second World War – in 1945 General Dwight D. Eisenhower and Field Marshal Bernard Montgomery attended a gala performance celebrating its conclusion. When the Troubles began in the late 1960s, the commercial centre of Belfast became a no-go zone. As Lyn Gallagher puts it in her history of the theatre, *The Grand Opera House, Belfast*:

'Throughout much of the seventies, the centre of Belfast

was eerily quiet at night. Few pubs remained open and few buses ran after nine o'clock. Belfast people chose to take their amusement in neighbourhoods where they felt safe, or in their own homes.'

The theatre struggled during this period; a short-lived attempt to give it a new lease of life as a cinema failed. In the early 1970s, there were plans for the building to be closed and sold to developers, but the Ulster Architectural Society mounted a campaign to save it, and in 1974 — days before the demolition was due to take place - it became the first listed building in Northern Ireland.

Being so close to the Europa Hotel, the Grand Opera House inevitably sustained bomb damage, first in 1991 and then, more seriously, in 1993, when it was targeted directly. A photograph from the time shows the side torn out of the building, its insides collapsing into the street, bowed and splintered, nearby bollards bent back by the blast. Fortunately, no one was injured, but the theatre was closed for many months. Soon after it reopened, in a display of resilience, the BAFTA celebrations were presented here in September 1994.

The doors are open from the foyer directly into the theatre. Standing over the road in the dark, I can gaze straight in to the auditorium, glittering like the exposed insides of a Fabergé egg, over the heads of the patrons, bustling into their seats and chatting as they wait for the show to begin. I have a discombobulating sense of being both part of this throng and outside of it. A poster nearby indicates what the audience is waiting for: Peter Corry's *The Call of The Celts*, 'a musical journey through some of the all-time favourite Celtic classics performed by one of the great voices to come out of Ireland.'

The doors snap shut. Tonight, I won't be going inside.

'Even before anything happens on stage, you are having a theatrical experience. You are in a Matcham theatre,' wrote Susan Hill in *The Spectator*, after a visit to his Everyman Theatre in Cheltenham.

The next morning, I am sitting in one of the boxes of the Grand Opera House with Head of Marketing, Simon Goldrick, gazing out at Matcham's auditorium. A gentle gradient of red velvet seats ascends beneath two sweeping gold balconies. The ornamentation displays a highly 'exotic' flourish; styles and cultural influences are clashed with abandon. Angels, prayer dials, monkeys, cherubim, elephant heads, cross-legged Indian gods, stars of David, mysterious scrolled lettering of no provenance; everything is gilded and brash, a dream space, too much for me to make sense of at one glance.

The 'imperial' aesthetic was characteristic of its time, and of much of Matcham's work. As Andrew Saint writes in his essay for the book *Frank Matcham & Co*:

'That theme, persistent in English culture throughout

Matcham's maturity, confers upon his hastily conceived décor a resonance that would otherwise be lacking. It develops out of Victoria's two jubilees in 1887 and 1897, rises to a first frenzy with the Boer War, and proceeds with growing anxiety to the social turmoil of the years 1911-13, and the naïve recruiting for the First World War. Many of those recruits, one may be sure, felt their hearts stir with patriotic loyalty while thrilling to some act against the loosely imperial backdrop of a Matcham theatre. Often, perhaps, his illusionistic scenarios fostered illusions.'

Now, the 'orientalism' of the place is a monument to a rather uncomfortable political era, and it is hard to divorce my perception of it from the knowledge that, at this moment in history, the controversial rule of the British Raj in India was at its height.

Matcham's approach was certainly not to everyone's taste at the time, and a certain snobbery is detectable in how his work was written about by his peers. Saint reports that *The Builder*, the architectural journal, only covered his works briskly and sniffily; Edwin Sachs wrote in his 1896 publication *Modern Opera Houses and Theatres*:

'There is no doubt ... that his plans have a certain individuality and that his scheme generally serves the unambitious purpose of the occupiers in a satisfactory manner. However, to fully illustrate such theatres in a volume dealing with theatre architecture in the best sense would be as anomalous as to include the 'jerry-builder's cottages' in volume on domestic architecture.'

What seems to have irked his contemporaries is a perceived lack of seriousness. His buildings were not rooted in academic discipline, but instead driven by pragmatic and commercial considerations; he mashed up styles, and his motivations were unashamedly showy and populist. Matcham, moreover, had not received formal training as an architect. He had been an apprentice to a London quantity surveyor and in a local architecture practice in his home town, Torquay, before taking up a job with the celebrated theatre architect J.T. Robinson. He married Robinson's daughter in 1877. When Robinson died the following year, Matcham inherited his practice. He was just 24 years old. Matcham took over Robinson's work on a project in the Elephant and Castle in London, and in 1879, his first theatre opened its doors.

His timing couldn't have been better. Matcham's arrival coincided with the great boom in theatre building that occurred during the Victorian era. The Theatres Act of 1843 had restricted the powers of the Lord Chamberlain to censor plays and, instead, granted local authorities the right to license playhouses, bringing to an end the monopoly of the Patent Theatres. Now, with a burgeoning urban population, and the great popularity of variety, theatres were thriving.

Furthermore, the new health and safety regulations of the late 1800s forced the closure of many of the old pub music halls, so new theatres were required to cater for demand.

The Grand Opera House was not just a place for theatrical performances. Gallagher's book contains an image of one of the theatre's original posters. Dated Monday 13th June 1898, it advertises the 'Grand Opening Night of the Summer Circus Season' and carries an illustration of a daredevil circus performer, standing astride three horses, whip raised in his hand. 'NOTICE — This Handsome Building can be transformed into a LUXURIOUS CIRCUS in the wonderful short space of 24 hours, being built for the above purpose, and adapted in every way for the FINEST CIRCUS AND NOVELTY PERFORMANCE EVER WITNESSED IN GREAT BRITAIN. The Season will be under the personal supervision of MR PEARCE BUTLER, the experienced up-to-date Manager and Ringmaster.'

Matcham's design featured a mechanical winch to lower the stage and a mechanism for broadening and raising the proscenium arch, giving a better view of the elephants and acrobats. He was known for his deployment of the latest technological developments, such as his introduction, elsewhere, of cantilevered balconies, which negated the need for pillars and thus greatly improved sightlines. An innovation on show here in Belfast was his ventilation system; seven gas burners in the roof heated the air, causing it to rise and be sucked out of the theatre.

Another invention to emerge from Matcham's office was the Panic Bolt, a mechanism that allowed for doors to be opened quickly and easily in an emergency, The Bolt was designed by his employee, Robert Alexander Briggs, who was horrified by the tragedy at Victoria Hall in Sunderland in 1883, when 183 children were crushed to death during a stampede at a magic show. He was determined it should never happen again.

Theatres are dangerous places. As I researched this book, I started jotting down a list of theatres that have burnt down. The Globe in 1613, when no one was harmed but a man's trousers were set on fire (he was saved by a friend who doused him with a flagon of beer). The Theatre Royal Exeter in 1887, the worst fire in British theatre history: 186 people were killed, many suffocating in the crush as they tried to escape the poorly designed exits from the cheap seats in the upper gallery. The list grew, over pages and pages. Some theatres didn't burn down just once. Take Glasgow's Theatre Royal, which has been situated on several sites over the last couple of centuries. It burnt down in 1829, 1840, 1849, 1863, 1879, 1956 and 1970. According to the Theatres Trust, in the mid to late 19th century the average life expectancy of a theatre was less than 20 years.

As new regulation began to come into force, Matcham was at the forefront of the drive towards improved safety in theatre buildings. At the Grand Opera House he installed features including tip-up seating, additional fire exits and an asbestos fire curtain. In theory, this auditorium could be cleared in three minutes, even at its original capacity of more than 2,500 (now it is a little over 1,000, with no substantive changes to layout).

Many of those additional audience members were working-class people, who crammed onto benches in 'The Gods'. They entered the theatre through a dedicated entrance. As Marvin Carlson notes in *Places of Performance*, 'Audience spaces have almost always reflected with accuracy the class preoccupations of their society'. As was typical of theatre architecture at the time, the entrance for the different tiers were kept apart, so the middle-class audience members could enjoy their evening without encountering anyone from the lower orders. It was a means of returning 'respectability' to an artform that had become, by the early 1800s, rather populist and rowdy. But Matcham's theatre ensured that everyone got a good view of the stage. His gift was not only for fitting as many bums on seats as possible, but also for providing great sightlines, regardless of how much (or little) you'd paid for your ticket.

What was the appeal of the Grand Opera House to

the various communities that packed this room to the rafters? Matcham's auditorium is somewhere set apart from the everyday, and would surely have seemed highly distinct from the dust and dirt of Victorian Belfast. Where much of contemporary theatre architecture seeks to draw people across the threshold into spaces that are homely or represent a continuation of the street, here audiences were meant to be impressed, perhaps a little awestruck. As Saint writes, 'The more brassily it was decorated, the better it supplied what the average punter missed in the drabness of his or her everyday life ... it responded to an emotional need which we no longer have.'

In the wake of the Good Friday Agreement, the arts had a significant role to play in peace building. Public subsidy increased and new venues opened their doors, such as The Mac Belfast and the Stirling Prize-shortlisted Lyric Theatre, down on the waterfront. But few have born witness to the years of conflict as the Grand Opera House has. It literally withstood everything this volatile period of history threw at it. "We think we're the only theatre in the country that has a blast wall," Goldrick comments.

The work staged here is on the most part fairly apolitical — West End musicals, ballet and amateur dramatics. Goldrick credits this neutrality with the continued importance of the theatre in the lives of those from both sides of the conflict. "Places like this became a refuge from the madness that was going on outside the doors, because it feels like its owned by everybody. It's part of the narrative, pre-Troubles, Troubles and post Troubles. It had a role to play in healing but also keeping the sanity of the city in the worst days," he tells me.

Tonight's fare, though, is an exception. Jake O' Kane's playing. He's a Northern Irish comic I've never heard of before, but is big news here, star of BBC Northern Ireland's *The Blame Game*. The house is packed, and Matcham's design sings. Although still opulent, when filled with people the auditorium attains an equilibrium of sorts — it is a room meant to be full. Stepping on stage, the warm-up act gazes out into the auditorium, then quips: "this is fucking posh — too posh for the likes of me".

Later, O' Kane, who is Catholic, asks the audience to identify their religious backgrounds. The different groups in the audience, Catholic and Protestant, cheer accordingly. It's a fairly even split. "Are there any Orange Men in?" he asks, and a chap in the row just in front of me raises his hand. "That's great, I can get a grant because you're here," O'Kane says. He takes the piss out of both sides equitably.

The Sandy Row mural comes in for special attention: "Catholics can't march, and Protestants can't paint". He displays the image of the paramilitary with the AK47 and points out the strange proportions of the face, how his mouth isn't quite where it ought to be. "He doesn't need a balaclava, he's terrifying enough as it is!" The auditorium boils with laughter.

Gazing up at the rows of beaming faces in Matcham's glittering tiers, I think of all this theatre — this city — has withstood. How delightful to share laughter in a place as absurd and eccentric as this.

6

LIVERPOOL EVERYMAN

Merseyside

Hailstones. Two cathedrals. Recycled school lab benches.
Paper, scissors, stone. Inverse velvet. 105 Liverpudlians.

AS I CONTINUED MY EXPLORATIONS of historic British theatres, a question was playing in the back of my mind. What makes a great theatre *today*? Reeling off a shopping list of elements you would want in a new theatre should be easy: good acoustics, decent sightlines, plentiful toilets, ease of access, high tech lighting and sound. But the nominations I received were far more varied than this logic would suggest. While some of my friends told me that they love dressing up for a night at a Grade II-listed venue in the West End, others preferred the rough and ready charms of a performance in a dank cellar on the Edinburgh Fringe. Others still eschewed the traditional venue altogether, spending their downtime getting lost in disused railway arches or abandoned factories. To focus on how comfortable the seats are, it was becoming clear, would be to miss the point. We come to know buildings, after all, not by their pediments and porticos, but by the role they play in our lives. How we live inside them.

This train of thought was leading me towards a somewhat more nebulous comprehension of a great theatre than that suggested by Vitruvius's architectural guidelines, or Matcham's insistence on opulence. I wanted to know how the term 'great theatre' might translate into something more concrete — and I imagined that visiting a theatre recently laurelled as the most important new building in the UK might provide me with some more substantial clues.

The Liverpool Everyman is on Hope Street, a thoroughfare that represents a meeting point for two different versions of Liverpool; on the edge of the Georgian heart of the city and leading down to Toxteth, a deprived area notorious for the riots of the 1980s and, more recently, the subject of several regeneration schemes. At either end of the street stand two cathedrals: the Anglican Liverpool Cathedral, designed by Giles Gilbert Scott, and the Roman Catholic Liverpool Metropolitan Cathedral, an uncompromisingly modern structure designed by Frederick Gibberd and affectionately nicknamed 'Paddy's Wigwam'. I arrive in the middle of a hailstorm. The street is a chiaroscuro of sunlight and icy shadow, and my breath chills on the air. Liverpool has the swept-out feeling of a cold, bright morning.

On first appearances, the Liverpool Everyman is rather an ordinary building: a wide box spread across five floors, its name alight in red neon letters and its frontage protected from the bleached light by rows of sunshades. Four brick chimneys project from the roof and call to mind a steamer ship; an echo of Liverpool's industrial past. A striking façade, certainly, but not a building designed to dominate a skyline or command the gaze. And, on first appearances, an unlikely candidate to win the RIBA Stirling Building of the Year, British architecture's most coveted silverware.

Yet, in 2014 it did precisely that, the first time a theatre had ever received the award. The competition included Renzo Piano's iconic Shard and Zaha Hadid's London Aquatics Centre, two structures of staggering ambition that seem designed to prompt, as Ayn Rand would have it, 'the peculiar solemnity of looking at the sky [that] comes, not from what one contemplates, but from that uplift of one's head.'

The human scale of the Liverpool Everyman, though, is its greatest virtue. Established in 1964, the Liverpool Everyman's first home was Hope Hall, a 19th-century chapel on this site that had become the meeting point for a collective of artists, poets and musicians, the doyens of the city's burgeoning bohemian scene. When it became a theatre, the emphasis was on plays by homegrown writers who reflected and celebrated working-class Liverpool life. Willy Russell's *Shirley Valentine* and *Stags and Hens* premiered here. The Everyman, as people are fond of recalling, was well-loved, with a welcoming vibe; you could just as easily turn up in a ball gown as not bother dressing up at all.

But the old chapel was crumbling and outdated, ill-fitted to the ambitions of a modern theatre. In 2010 the Liverpool Everyman's leadership team — artistic director Gemma Bodinetz and executive director Deborah Aydon — engaged architects Haworth Tompkins to deliver the scheme for the new building. The name of this north London architecture practice has, in recent times, become synonymous with pretty much any exciting new theatre development; in the last few years, they've revitalised the National Theatre and the Young Vic, and they're hard at work on projects at Battersea Arts Centre, Bristol Old Vic and the Theatre Royal, Drury Lane. But the Liverpool Everyman stands, for now, as their crowning glory.

I step through the plate glass doors into the foyer. The floors are arranged in tiers; windows and doorways open out to the stairwell. A muted palette of concrete, tarnished steel and burgundy paintwork that visual artist Antoni Malinowski has decorated with abstract patterns — a series of vermillion blotches and bronze flecks, suggestive of a shoal of fish or a stream of blood cells.

This is a building to be explored. The floors are arranged at half levels and have a suggestive theatricality, the architecture offering impromptu stages and miniature proscenium arches, framing momentary pedestrian dramas. The consideration with which everyday materials have been used is transformative: concrete walls imprinted with wooden strapping to soften them; reinforced glass turned at an angle; bar-tops fashioned from school science lab benches. I'd like to run my hands over the surfaces. What's more, I feel I may. The word used about this building again and again is 'patina'; the beauty of its elements will deepen, not diminish, with wear, acquiring new texture through human touch.

Robert Longthorne, building development director, takes me on a tour. The aesthetic extends into the backstage areas; spaces so often unloved and unlovely are treated, here, with the same consideration as front-of-house. Subdued but not characterless, decorated with grey paintwork and plywood that is quintessentially Haworth Tompkins, these spaces are softer than the harsh black box of the conventional rehearsal room. We visit a suite of offices on the top floor: an education studio, a workshop and a writers' room whose desks overlook the foyer and are visible to passersby. "If we can improve the lot of writers by helping audiences understand how much work goes into creating a play, so much the better," Longthorne tells me.

On the day the Stirling Prize committee visited, the Liverpool Everyman was hosting a 'Fun Palace'. A free, nationwide celebration of arts and sciences, Fun Palaces encourages venues to invite their local community to take over the building and stage whatever performances and activities they like in it. So rather than enjoying an uninterrupted experience of the architecture's carefully considered details, the Prize committee encountered children making gingerbread men in the café. Big flowers crafted from sugar paper decorated the banisters. A man with a swimming hat was reciting Shakespeare soliloquies while having his head iced like a cake.

Elsewhere people were experiencing the therapeutic benefits of a 'gong bath'. In reality, it showed the building off at its very best. As RIBA president Stephen Hodder wrote, 'the success of this exceptional new building lies in the architect's close involvement with the local community throughout the project.' This is important not only because all civic buildings might reasonably be thought to benefit from co-creation with the community that will use them, but because it points to the unique role theatres have to play in modern society.

"A common aspiration for all of the work is, what is the point of a theatre? You're going to spend £30 million on a public cultural building. It's not just so the sightlines are good and you can put on *Oklahoma!*" architect Steve Tompkins tells me later, when I meet him one baking afternoon in his offices on the top floor of an old warehouse in Kentish Town.

This isn't the first time our paths have crossed. I met Tompkins in the late '90s, when I was 13 or 14 years old. I was a member of the Theatre Royal Bath Young People's Theatre, and his practice had just been commissioned to create what would become the first purpose-built young people's theatre in the country, in the recently acquired building adjoining the main house. I remember sitting on the floor in a circle, as a big white sheet of paper was laid out in the middle. We each took one of the chunky marker pens offered to us. "Right," he said.

"What do you want your theatre to be like?" Children love to play this game, drawing fantastical buildings they hope to inhabit in their future, constructions with looping roof-to-garden waterslides, chocolate swimming pools and docks for their hovercraft. Although I was by that point rather old for it, in my memory that moment contains the lustre of a crafts session, letting loose with the Pritt Stick and Crayola.

The resulting theatre finally opened in 2005 in the husk of the old Robin's cinema where I'd spent my preteen years slurping buckets of Coke and watching Leonardo di Caprio films. Inside the cinema's crumbling Bath stone walls, a 120-seat, oval-shaped auditorium had been suspended. A delightful, miniature playing space called *the egg*, it featured many of the ideas sparked in that session: a sound-proofed room with glass frontage and a P.A., from where parents with crying babies could enjoy the show without disturbing other people; a stage area in the café for impromptu pop-up performances.

A few months after it opened, a group of us decided we wanted to stage an arts festival to raise funds for former child soldiers in Uganda. Unquestioningly, the directors handed us the keys and let us get on with it. In the rooftop rehearsal room, with floor-to-ceiling windows with views across the city, we developed a play based on a Ugandan myth. A couple of weeks later it headlined our festival on the stage downstairs. In the cafe, there was a post-show discussion with political experts, an art exhibition and a band who played rock covers late into the evening. The event sold out and we duly dispatched a cheque to a Ugandan charity.

So it had come to pass. We had sketched out the building we would, in time, occupy. How extraordinarily privileged we were. I doubt Tompkins and the team at the Theatre Royal Bath appreciate the extent to which that communicated to a group of young people that the future really did belong to them, that they could make of it what they wished.

"We often say that theatres are one of the few places where a whole cross-section of society can come together in the same space, in peace, and experience the same version of their common humanity being played out back to them," Tompkins says to me. I am struck by how exactly he has encapsulated my own beliefs about the role of theatre. Throughout our conversation I find myself agreeing vigorously with almost everything he says, interjecting to voice my enthusiasm and to solicit his approval of my own preoccupations and prejudices.

It is only later, listening to my Dictaphone recording and cringing at my lousy interview technique, that I understand that the alignment of our views is no coincidence. I've learnt about the artform in settings crafted by Tompkins and his team, first at *the egg* in Bath and then at London's Royal Court and Battersea Arts Centre.

A phrase keeps coming back to me from theatre-maker

Chris Goode's book *The Forest and The Field*: 'At its best, you can live inside theatre, in the way you might feel you live inside a set of political and religious commitments: the feeling that you don't contain such commitments, they contain you ... theatre's what I think with.'

An auditorium has an aura you sense as soon as you step inside it. It seems intangible, almost alchemical, and yet it is the work of a thousand subtle choices: the fabric covering the seats; the colour of the paintwork; which entrance you used. Tompkins describes the auditorium as 'an incredibly finely calibrated tool, like a cabinet maker's plane, something that has grown through use, through practice, through endlessly repeated attempts to hone it and tweak it into something that has an intrinsic rightness'. A good auditorium can make a half empty seating rake seem half full, a mediocre play sing.

I enter through a set of double doors into the stalls, then take the stairs and find my seat in the balcony that wraps around three walls on the upper level. The fact that the audience enters collectively, through the same entrance, is another deliberate choice that communicates the ethics of the organisation, and a counter to the heritage of theatre architecture that is designed to keep different classes apart. If you think of the theatre as a communal space then its architecture bears a democratic responsibility to provide a level playing field, where the presence of each individual is valued and upheld.

At the Liverpool Everyman today, the auditorium is laid out 'in the round', with four banks of seating on each side of the stage. The playing space is enormous, 10 metres square, and would more typically be presented in a thrust configuration, a layout inherited from the old chapel. Exposed terracotta brickwork warms the space; around 25,000 bricks were reclaimed from the old building in order to reduce the development's carbon footprint. There is no escaping the fact that theatres are dreadful for the environment — with power guzzling lighting rigs, vast quantities of flyers and posters that end up in the bin, and sets that get scrapped at the end of a run. "If you're spending however many hundred tonnes of carbon on a building it had better be worth it," Tompkins tells me. "An imperative for us was for the building to be a sustainable exemplar — and then I think that idea dovetailed quite happily with the idea of humble materials, the reuse of a demolished building." The bricks bring into the room a trace of what was here before, and perhaps these stones really do have memories, are imprinted with what played out here in the past. Tompkins and I discuss the affection that theatre people have for ghost stories. "How much of it is autosuggestion, an internal emotional landscape you take to a place? But that is valid, I think, if you take that sense of relish for the authenticity of something that happened in the past then of course you're going to be in a more heightened state ... whether there's actually anything in the ether, who knows."

I imagine it is beyond the ken of the 399 screaming primary school kids surrounding me that Haworth Tompkins deliberately laid the velvet on the seats upside down, so when they sit on them the pile is roughed up rather than smoothed, imprinted with their presence. But as I watch them before the show begins — playing *Paper, scissors, stone*, eating snacks, daring each other to dart onto the stage to touch the set — it's evident they feel at home.

The matinee show today is a play about four children from different corners of the globe, meeting in their dreams on a quest to save a storytelling giant. A huge tree spans the stage — it is a library, a climbing frame and, later, the roof of the sky, scattered with fairy light stars. Anyone who feels remotely cynical about theatre should go and watch a play with a bunch of children; they are the perfect audience, unguarded and responsive, emitting peals of laughter, squealing in delight at the word 'fart', picking up threads of dialogue from the stage and joining in. They make noise, noise not usually permitted in theatre and yet which the best theatres do more than contain — they thrive on it, because it's a way of saying *we're all here*.

After the performance, I step out, blinking, into the bright afternoon light. I look up at the shutters on the front of the building. Peering closer, I notice they are adorned with a series of portraits. 105 ordinary Liverpool people. They turn and tilt in the sun, shimmering, Pointillist figures punched into aluminium sheets. The main entrance is on the west façade. Following the building's religious heritage and the proximity of the two cathedrals, the team had been researching the west fronts of churches and the larger-than-life size statuary arraigned on them. When it was established that this elaborate sunshade would be required for the building to meet its green aspirations, the solution became "obvious", as Tompkins tells me. Following a public call-out, thousands of local people turned up to have their portrait taken by photographer Dan Kenyon. "The only stipulation was they couldn't be famous." Ultimately, these were whittled down to this final selection of images that reflected the diversity of Liverpool.

"It seemed like there was complete open-heartedness to the idea ... it's a statement of intent about the purpose and meaning of the building, apart from anything else. And of course, gives you the architectural presence and texture that you need."

This group of people can be seen to represent anyone in the Liverpool community. Like the eponymous hero of the *Everyman* morality play, they are a cypher for the experiences common to all humankind. On the other hand, it's a specific group of individuals, and the story of this façade will alter with the weft and weave of their lives — already two children have been born who appeared in the original photos *in utero*, and one individual has died.

I've long thought, lazily, of architecture and theatre as being distinct disciplines, pulling in opposite directions. Architecture is preoccupied with posterity, built to withstand the span of a human life — of many lives; while theatre is a mortal, fleeting thing, possessed for a slippery instant, always rushing towards its own end. Somehow, these impulses are reconciled in the Liverpool Everyman. Most of Haworth Tompkins' work has not been to design brand new theatres but, rather, to breathe new life into existing ones, some many centuries old. This process has shaped an acute awareness of how time works on a building. Even in their early works, they sought a kind of 'rigorous harmony' between new and old, and this made the relationship between the practice and its clients a particularly sympathetic one. "It became obvious that theatre practice was also fundamentally about time, about temporality, about the moment, about continuity," says Tompkins. The sense you have is not so much a building but an organism, fitted for evolution and adaptation to changing atmospheric pressures. It carries its past with it while also straining to the future, a creature of the modern world that is unpredictable and larger than the purview of any individual.

There are political problems associated with building theatres. It cost £27 million to construct the Liverpool Everyman, and whatever its avowed democratic principles, a building of this expense and scale must be in some way beholden to the capitalist system within which it operates. As academic Juliet Rufford writes in *Theatre and Architecture*, 'the way we see and understand staged events depends, to a great extent, on how they are framed and presented'. A building almost inevitably establishes power structures; someone, after all, has the keys and decides who comes in and out, what goes on the stage, and what doesn't. And however much work an organisation may do to overcome them, a theatre inherently proposes a set of associations that are, to some, alienating — because in many instances theatre has become the preserve of a narrow strata of society. Regardless of the careful consideration given to the materials used in the handrails, there are those who may simply never make it across the threshold. It's no coincidence that many of the most interesting, inclusive theatre projects, particularly in recent years, have been staged outside and in spaces not designated for theatre, as I'll explore later in this book.

But just as Haworth Tompkins' architecture has been enriched by borrowing from theatre's sense of temporality, I think the permanence of buildings dedicated to performance enriches theatre too. We need places to return to, and if not theatres, where, now, may our public selves be tethered, when so much public space has become privatised? Over time, a theatre should mellow into its landscape, learn how to speak in the vernacular. The proposition is a long-term relationship, and a narrative develops that transcends any single show. And because the lifespan of a building is likely to extend beyond that of any individual, the theatre comes, more than anything, to belong to a *place*.

When a theatre works well, as the Liverpool Everyman surely does, it reflects the city back at itself: not only as it is, but at its best, when space is a thing to be shared, not protected — when different ideas and lifestyles are met with openness and curiosity. As he explains to me, Tompkins wanted to build "something that made the city a better place, that made the people of Liverpool walk taller and with a spring in their step".

7

BATTERSEA ARTS CENTRE

London

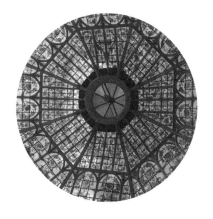

*A black cat. Jerusalem. Damn Good Coffee. A clutch of
irises. An omelette. A paper house.*

ON 13TH MARCH 2015, I was on a train heading southwest from Waterloo station. As we passed through Clapham, I glanced in the direction of Battersea Arts Centre, which can just be made out in the distance from that railway line. The blue air was filled with smoke, thick and heavy on the skyline. It seemed implausible, the contents of a disordered dream. But a scan of Twitter confirmed it: Battersea Arts Centre was on fire.

Artistic director David Jubb learned the news at home on the Kent coast. His colleague made what seemed to be a routine phone call to inform him that the building's fire alarms had gone off and that the staff had assembled outside — the sort of thing that happens in theatres when people burn their toast or use the wrong kind of fog machine in a rehearsal room. But then he heard the catch in her throat as she saw flames take hold of the roof of the Grand Hall at the back of the building. The panic rose in her voice when she told him to get here right away.

Within minutes the fire was raging, wind stoking the flames and spreading it across the roof, towards the clock tower. There is some mesmerising quality to a fire which makes people stop in their tracks, unable to turn their gaze from the astonishing force with which it takes hold, spreads and consumes. Crowds gathered behind flimsy red and white tape, training their cameras on it, tilting their phones up towards this grim, impromptu tourist attraction. A round attic window at the back funnelled the blaze into the sky, furious and alive. Two firemen were raised up on an aerial ladder platform, tiny black figures lifting a high, fizzing arc of water towards the flames, absurdly inadequate. Soon, the roof caved in, the inferno opening up the building's insides to the sky, everything leaning inwards and disintegrating, beams and tiles and scaffolding poles. "Jesus have mercy God," someone said.

As he rode up to the city, Jubb watched the fire on Twitter, his phone flickering with intermittent WiFi signal. Stepping off the train at Clapham Junction, he smelt wood burning and knew it was his own building. When he reached the crest of Lavender Hill, he looked in the opposite direction, as if in fear that, unshielded by his mobile phone, he would also be caught.

What was it that was becoming so much ash, lifted on the thick London air and scattered across the city? The tangible things, certainly: ornate coving, the rare Victorian organ. Nobody was hurt in the fire, but for some time it was feared that Pluto, the theatre's much-loved black cat, had been caught inside — until he turned up days later, brazen and unharmed.

It struck me, once the flames were dampened, that a burnt-out building becomes a kind of aide-memoire for all the things that happened inside it. The impulse was to remember, and in the days that followed, people began to tell stories that demonstrated all that BAC had meant to them. Someone spoke of riding a bike around the Grand Hall, chasing balloons; another of being moved to tears by the spoken word artist Kate Tempest, ferocious and vital as she told stories of everyday gods. On Twitter, a hashtag started — #BACPhoenix — and very quickly it was flooded with stories of days and nights spent at BAC, debates sparked and worldviews changed, friends made and romances kindled. For many, many people, the venue was part of their psychological cartography of the city, a coordinate from which they'd mapped their lives. 'It's quite astonishing how much of your heart you can give to a place,' wrote theatre journalist Catherine Love, as if a physical fragment of her had been held there, locked into the walls.

Battersea Arts Centre carries my stories too. If the Theatre Royal Bath was where I had my first experience of theatre, this was where I fine-tuned my tastes. I was unhappy and broke when I arrived in the city at 19; desperately casting around for something to cling on to, I found BAC. I started coming to free evening classes as a means of escaping my miserable flat and painful relationship, and for a few hours I'd get lost in whatever creative project was on offer that week. I remember writing a poem about the clientele of the furniture shop where I worked. A stand-up comedy class. One night, with a bunch of new friends I had made, I plotted the downfall of Rupert

Murdoch's media empire (alas, I have forgotten the precise details, but the friendships remain). I didn't speak to anyone I met about the fact that I was frightened to go home, but the simple grace of knowing there was a place where my presence, and voice, were valued, was sustaining. I'd found my tribe.

At BAC I began to comprehend the full scope of what theatre can be. Theatre, I was discovering, encompassed a sphere of activity far vaster than I had yet imagined. There were performances where audience members were blindfolded and pushed about in wheelchairs, had their feet washed, or were suspended out of second-floor windows. Once I watched a group of women, so inspired by the fearless feminist performance they had just seen, get up on stage, remove their clothes and perform the chorus of 'Jerusalem'. Once, I cooked a meal with people I didn't know in a room on the top floor; over dinner, we talked about the people we had broken bread with in our lives, and I saw how you can make a family of strangers. The artists that BAC hosted seemed to give so much more of themselves than I was used to, and so the audiences gave more of themselves too. Often, the exchanges overflowed the official bounds of the show, conversations prompted by the work carried on in the bar, debates raging until the last order bell.

There were parties here too. I dressed up as a pirate and as Wednesday Adams. Once, I stayed up all night, watching back-to-back episodes of *Twin Peaks* and drinking mugs of Damn Good Coffee. How often I've stumbled out drunk on to Lavender Hill, carved a lunging, wheeling path down to the station just in time to catch the last train back to whatever far-flung corner of the city I was calling home. Twice, I was kissed. Nothing came of those kisses. They stand alone; lovely jewels of the night.

The thing about BAC is that it isn't actually a theatre at all. The organisation was established in 1979 in Battersea's Old Town Hall, a striking building designed by architect E.W. Mountford, who was responsible for numerous other local buildings including Lavender Hill Library, just over the road, as well as Sheffield Town Hall and the Old Bailey.

The Grand Hall at the back of the building contained the fire, so approaching up Lavender Hill, there is no immediate sign of damage. I am greeted by a broad red Suffolk brick façade, dressed in Bath stone. A relief depicts the Battersea coat of arms, upheld by Prudence and Justice, and the Young Borough — shown as an anxious toddler — being instructed by figures representing Art and Literature. Three stone balconies at first-floor level — adjacent to one of the main performance spaces — suggest that the drama contained might brim over at any point, spill out into the lives of those who are now passing by. A tower is domed in greened copper and a weather vane carries the year it opened: 1893.

This is an impressive building, the municipal dream of another era. Built by the fledgling local authority of Battersea — only officially established in 1889 — the expensive flourishes, such as those detailed reliefs, attest to the burgeoning sense of civic pride in this working-class corner of the city. The area was becoming synonymous with radical left-wing politics, earning it the epithet 'Red' Battersea. In 1892, leading radical John Burns had been elected as MP; he was one of the first working-class men to be a cabinet minister, until he resigned his post in 1914 in protest against Britain's involvement in the First World War. In 1913, John Archer became Britain's first black mayor, saying in his victory speech, 'they will look to Battersea and say Battersea has done many things in the past, but the greatest thing it has done has been to show that it has no racial prejudice and that it recognises a man for the work he has done'. The borough's motto was *Non Mihi, Non Tibi, Sed Nobis*. 'Not for me, not for you, but for us.'

When Battersea was merged with its neighbouring borough of Wandsworth in 1965, the town hall became obsolete. In 1979, after some time as a council-run venue, the building was turned into an independent arts centre. Although Mountford envisaged the Grand Hall itself as a platform for 'high-class entertainments for the people of Battersea', the town hall was never intended as a theatre.

No space in the building was designed specifically for a stage, and so every corner of it might become one. Often the most interesting performances take place in attic rooms, offices or corridors, the location shaping the drama to its own contours. BAC — more than any other theatre I know, I think — has a kind of active presence in the drama; it almost seems to become a character in its own right, with its own desires, even in conflict with the intentions of the artist.

Throughout its years as an arts centre, BAC has continued to be a staging ground for the civic life of the borough too: a venue for weddings, tea dances, Slimming World meetings and blood donor clinics. This history is surely the wellspring of the grief that followed the fire. BAC is more than a theatre; it is a place where people have been named, votes cast, lives commemorated, the identity of the borough stitched together by the threads that unspooled through these double doors and out into Lavender Hill. We understand buildings not merely as a series of lines and planes, but through the roles they play in our lives. Which is why so many shiny new buildings fail; they are not suited to the messiness of being human.

At the time of the fire, Haworth Tompkins had already begun to redevelop the site. They had pursued a way of working that chimed with BAC's own 'scratch' approach to making theatre — in which rough, early versions of shows are presented to audiences, developing to full production in response to their feedback — so that rather than approaching the building with a fixed idea of what they wanted the final product to be like, they tested prototypes of their plans, shaping their work and responding to performances. BAC's woodburning stoves, for instance, are the legacy of 2007's show, *The Masque of the Red Death*, an epic immersive production by Punchdrunk based on the Edgar Allan Poe story. Haworth Tompkins opened up the old hearths of the old town hall, enabling some scenes to be lit by the evocative glow of firelight. In this way Haworth Tompkins' work has responded to the blanket of emotional sediment that lies thick here, shifting and resettling around the footfall of all those that traverse it.

I step through the double doors into the foyer, which is calm and quiet, just a distant burble of conversation spilling out of the café, the faint, high outline of The Beach Boys' 'Wouldn't It Be Nice'. Having this place to yourself for a few moments is a privilege. I gaze up at the marble staircase ascending before me, splitting at a mezzanine before sweeping up to an arcade, flooded with sun from the glass ceiling above. Underfoot is the intricate blue and white mosaic floor, a pattern of oversized worker bees, their wings spread. Somewhere away to my right, behind a set of firmly bolted metal doors, is where the Grand Hall once stood; where it is beginning, now, to be built again.

A quirk of the layout of Battersea Arts Centre means that

the Grand Hall is located around a corner from the rest of the building and down a hill, and therefore has always felt strangely concealed. You would get lost in a maze of corridors, passing endless rooms populated with ghostly dust motes, and then arrive in it, abruptly, where it didn't quite seem it should be. When I meet Jubb, later, he describes it as "almost sci-fi, like the Tardis ... you have no idea that in the midst of this warren of rooms is this vast-scale, glorious Victorian room" — speaking in the present tense, as if not yet acquainted with its loss. It *was* huge — accommodating up to 600 people — and in 1901 a large pipe organ was added, designed by celebrated organ builder Robert Hope-Jones, to ensure it was equipped to deliver the calibre of entertainment the local community deserved.[1] I remember that organ. I remember the highly polished wooden floors, the intricate plasterwork and the 1930s balcony where I once quietly watched a wild ceilidh unfurling beneath me.

In the wake of the blaze, a terrible beauty was to be found in the wreckage. Things at once familiar and disfigured, stretched out of shape by the heat or charred beyond recognition. Strange mottled fragments of paintwork, shed skin. Metalwork prematurely turned rust red, twisted into

---

[1] The organ was partially saved from the fire, as the mechanism was being restored off-site — sadly, the console, pipes and case were lost.

snaked ribbons. Globules of unidentifiable melted plastic like discarded chewing gum.

Artist Jake Tilson spent weeks on site, scanning the debris with the eye of a beachcomber and salvaging what he could. He collected isolated pieces of flotsam and placed them on plinths against white backdrops. In the book of photographs he took of these articles, they seem like museum exhibits — artefacts from a past age that have taken on the patina of things long buried: a fresnel lantern, a gauze, a pair of sunglasses. A gap had opened between us and our everyday stuff; the fire gave it new meaning, transforming ordinary objects into things rare and special.

This is, after all, what we do. We search the cinders for sense. The wreckage seemed to magnify modest acts of generosity: a gift of daffodils from a passerby; the local café owner who refused to charge when the BAC staff team took over his café for a six-hour emergency meeting. There were bigger things too. The Southbank Centre offered a home to Gecko's show *Missing*, which had been running in the Grand Hall; they performed an unplugged version, stripped of set and tech. The public contributed £75,000 in a few days, and the Government awarded a direct grant of £1 million. Just 24 hours later, the front half of the building had been declared safe and BAC reopened for performances of two shows.

After several weeks, David Jubb felt able, finally, to look

at the Grand Hall. What struck him was how the destruction had been contained, as if, he said, the Grand Hall "had sacrificed itself to save the rest of the building". The tide of wreckage was banked up against an immense wooden beam, blackened and gnarled by the intense heat. Beyond it, the adjacent bar area appeared to be untouched. A table and chair stood where they'd been left, chair slightly pushed back, the only suggestion there might have been an interruption. On the table lay a programme and a half-full glass of gin and tonic. As if at any moment normal service would be resumed: tickets ripped, beginners called, and the evening's entertainment begun.

I have been invited to spend the night at BAC. Theatres often express a desire to be considered 'a second home', but here that's quite literally the case. In one wing, eight individually designed bedrooms provide accommodation for artists who live here for up to three months at a time, while making new work in the building. My room, designed by artist Tom de Freston, is in the basement — decorated with a dark, messy pallet of splattered greys and blues, like a troubled night sky. Pasted to the walls are hundreds of tiny photographs of a bloodied white figure, without eyes or a mouth, like a character from a Guillermo del Toro movie. The room is apparently inspired by Act Four Scene Six of *King Lear*, in which the Earl of Gloucester attempts suicide. Not somewhere I'd want to stay for more than one night.

I dump my bags and sneak up into the balcony of what was once the Council Chamber of the town hall. Tonight the room is packed for a fundraising event for those affected by the terrible, fatal fire that happened at Grenfell Tower four nights ago. It is a sick time to be in the world, bad news coming in relentless, engulfing crashes. In the last month there have been terrorist attacks in Manchester and at London Bridge, and not long ago at Westminster. This morning a man in a white van drove into worshippers at a mosque in Seven Sisters.

Two days out from summer solstice, the city is baking hot — one of the hottest June weeks in over 40 years — and everything feels out of joint. In the Council Chamber, everyone is sweating, stripped back to damp white T-shirts and tiny cotton dresses, chugging through pint after pint of BAC's own brand lager. The bill is made up of a bunch of properly socialist comedians and the fare is caustic. They are targeting a reckless system that values profit over people. The fire at BAC was nothing like the fire at Grenfell, where 71 people died; a senseless, unnecessary loss. At BAC, not a single person suffered even a single scratch. If there's anything that they share, it's the evidence that a building is so much smaller than a human life. It shouldn't take fires to remind us.

Afterwards, I sit at the bar, drinking with one of the

producers as the venue empties around us. Pluto has caught a mouse, and we watch a duty manager make a half-hearted attempt to rescue it with a broom, before giving up and letting the cat disappear with its prey. I head back to my room. It's late and I'm quite tipsy. In a yellow kitchen, decorated with Van Gogh prints and a clutch of irises in a glass vase, I find two poets cooking an omelette and listening back to covers of old jazz songs they've recorded themselves playing during the day. I take hold of it all — the smell of onions, the bright colours of the flowers, 'The Girl from Ipanema' echoing through the empty corridors.

A few days later I join a small group of staff members on a tour of the construction work. We don hard hats and hi-viz jackets, traipse down Town Hall Road and in through a security gate. Inside, the builders have covered the floors in concrete and the vast space is filled with functional scaffolding, giving it the feel of an industrial warehouse.

Haworth Tompkins' refurbishment of the Grand Hall was almost complete when the fire happened. They were forced to begin again. How frustrating it must have been, like your computer crashing the night before an assignment is due and having to redo all your work, to the power of a million. Should they attempt to restore the Grand Hall exactly as it was, or take the opportunity to create something brand new: a high spec, purpose-built theatre, capable of delivering anything a 21st-century production requires? Ultimately, they arrived at a solution that sits somewhere between the two, a design that retains the best of the old Hall without paying it undue deference. The new timber lattice ceiling recalls the aesthetic of the beautiful plasterwork lost in the fire, but the 15-metre apex of the roof above will be opened up, with a new tech gallery. The organ will be restored and returned, but to a new location up on the balcony. The burnt patches of discolouration will remain in all their unsettling beauty, a legible trace of the fire which, like the weddings and the tea dances, has now become a chapter in the story of the building.

Suddenly, from nowhere, a flurry of grey wings; a bird swoops down through the metal bars of the scaffolding and alights, for a moment, on a ladder. The phoenix has become the symbol of BAC's recovery from the fire. When the Grand Hall reopens, it will be with *I'm a Phoenix Bitch* by Bryony Kimmings, a beautiful, brilliant performance artist who I believe more closely resembles the fabulous creature with fiery wings than any other.

But this bird is a pigeon: unglamorous but resilient. I like to think of the pigeon taking possession of the Grand Hall, nesting somewhere in the rafters. "They're a nightmare. They shit everywhere," our tour guide says, as it takes off, flies upwards into the space where the lights will be.

The philosopher J.L. Austin wrote that when we speak, our intention is not always to describe something. Sometimes, language can be an action, bringing about a tangible change in the world — like a promise, or a bet. He called these types of speech 'performative utterances'. This concept strikes me as pertinent to those testimonies in the days after the fire, because those sharing their stories were doing more than simply expressing their sense of loss. If a place is so much more than its bricks, if it is in fact the vast network of associations and memories tied to it, far knottier than anyone could ever hope to unpick, then it needs its stories to survive. What we were doing, as we reminisced in pubs across the city, updated our blogs and Facebook pages, was renewing BAC's existence — laying the keystone from which the very act of rebuilding might begin. Not summoning ghosts, but breathing life into the building again, gifting it back to itself.

The story I give to the Grand Hall is this. An October afternoon in 2009, reeled in from the depths of my memory, slippery and glistening. In this room, for Abigail Conway's *Home Sweet Home*, a paper town was being created. A huge map had been laid down, covering almost the entire floor. It loosely followed the geography of the local area — the layout of the main streets and the curve of the river. There were familiar landmarks: the power station, BAC itself, rendered in cardboard. But mostly it was space, left wide open for us to pitch homes and create a miniature metropolis of our own.

I chose a plot with a view of the Shard in the distance and started creating a dwelling from the flat-packed kit I'd been given — a tall, narrow affair reminiscent of the Georgian crescent houses of my hometown. I coloured it in with purple felt tip and sprinkled the roof with glitter. All around me, a community was springing up. My neighbours were hard at work on their own plots: a cottage covered in buttons; an art gallery with a silver roof made of tin foil; a diner with a natty houndstooth hoarding.

As we worked, we talked about what we wanted our town to be. We named our street and made plans for a park for the children to play in. We debated the potential impact of a brothel that had opened nearby, discussed how best to deal with the suspected theft of an unusual water feature (an empty Evian cap) from someone's garden. In the evening, we threw a party. We drank warm white wine from plastic cups and toasted the impromptu community we had created. I remember dancing to music from a tinny sound system. Then, far more quickly than we had assembled it, we dismantled our town, bid one another farewell and carried our homes off with us into the night.

The Grand Hall may have burnt down, but that paper house — I keep it with me still. It fits in the palm of my hand. Sometimes I feel that I live inside it.

8

MORECAMBE WINTER GARDENS THEATRE

Lancashire

A tortoiseshell butterfly. A rumbling stomach.
White noise. A hurtling glass. Jack the Ripper.
Eric Morecambe.

STORIES HELD IN STONES. There is something unsettling about the notion. Thinking about it, I remember T.C. Lethbridge's ideas about the existence of ghosts. Stone Tape theory, which he promoted, holds that under certain conditions emotionally charged events can imprint themselves on their surroundings, becoming locked into physical materials such as stone or wood to be replayed like a shaky video recording to terrified onlookers in the future.

Theatres are full of ghost stories: jilted lovers, disappointed performers, murdered audience members. At one London theatre, a disembodied head appears in full clown makeup. At another, a phantom dolphin is still whistling and backflipping decades after it expired in a tank beneath the stage. As a teenager at the Theatre Royal Bath, I became obsessed with the story of the spirit of Reg Maddox, a theatre producer who died suddenly of a heart attack during a rehearsal for the 'Butterfly Ballet' scene of the 1948 pantomime. On the opening night, a company member saw a live tortoiseshell butterfly backstage; it has materialised on numerous occasions since, often during the pantomime, and appears to bring good luck to whoever has spotted it. Although I never caught a glimpse of the butterfly-spirit myself, throughout my years hanging around the rehearsal studios and dressing rooms I was always half-primed for its appearance, my ears pricked for the beating of phantom, gossamer wings.

"The time is out of joint," the philosopher and hauntologist Jacques Derrida was wont to say, quoting *Hamlet*. Time has a particular slipperiness in the theatre. After all, in the theatre at least three temporal planes co-exist: that of the play's creation; that of the play's action; and the plane the audience currently inhabits. Do the onlookers think, too, about the future, coming all too soon, when the play will have disappeared, existing nowhere but memory? A window is opened through which ghosts might find passage.

Investigating this understanding of performance by signing up for an all-night ghost hunt at one of the most haunted theatres in Britain may be rather literal. Nevertheless, here I am, equipped with torch, sturdy footwear and my friend Honour, who has agreed to come and hold my hand. I want to understand why it is that theatres have such a strong association with ghosts. And I also fancy the idea of running amok in an abandoned theatre, freaking myself out with things that go bump in the night.

Even in the height of summer, Morecambe is empty. We check in at a B&B with a huge bay window overlooking the sand flats that stretch for eight miles towards the fells and mountains of the Lake District. As the sun sets, we watch the fading light change the flats through pearly whites, lavenders and ochres. The sand flats, and the waters in which they constantly shift, are treacherous. In 2004 at least 21 undocumented Chinese cockle pickers drowned after being stranded by the turning tide. The bay appears now as a placid, golden plain. But as we watch, the tide comes flooding back in, creeping fast across the sand and into the wormlike gulleys and rivulets; its surface is worried by currents that tug in different directions, quickly turning the water into a seething mass.

When dusk has fallen, we step out on to the promenade and walk towards the theatre, past boarded-up hotels and empty pubs. In its heyday in the early 20th century, Morecambe was a thriving resort, dubbed the Naples of the North. Grainy vintage photos show holidaymakers in heavy Edwardian dress promenading on the town's two piers; an art deco lido full of bathers; glamorous women participating in the annual Miss Great Britain contest. These amenities have long since disappeared, the piers succumbing to fire and storm and the lido to the attritions of town planning.

One of the principal attractions of that era was the Morecambe Winter Gardens on the seafront. In 1897, the Victoria Pavilion Theatre was added to an existing leisure complex containing a ballroom, billiards room, aquarium and seawater swimming baths. For many years it was a thriving entertainment hub, playing host to Vera Lynn, Charlie Chaplin and The Rolling Stones. It is one of few remaining music halls of this scale and quality from the era. But, like so many of England's seaside resorts, the gentle charms of Morecambe proved no match for the allure of cheap package holidays in the sun; by 1977 diminishing audiences had forced the theatre to close.

The ballroom has long since been demolished, but the theatre remains, a huge *memento mori* of past glories. In the gloaming, the red-brick structure dominates the prospect at the southern flank of the bay. Its scrolled gable seems to glow against the crepuscular sky. Two square towers thrust skywards at either end of the building. A balcony runs along the width of the first floor, and above it stands a huge, semicircular window, three storeys high, surrounded by stark ornamentation with the appearance of so many teeth. In the turrets, clusters of weeds have taken root, cracking the brickwork, an intimation that these stones will someday crumble away entirely. But still, we feel dwarfed, as if entering this building means encountering something far bigger than ourselves. No doubt we're meant to.

In the theatre's Parisian Bar, we find our fellow ghost hunters — a group of about 25 people clad in practical warm clothing, sipping squash and tea from polystyrene cups and chatting animatedly. Some are in couples, others with their parents and siblings ready to enjoy a family night out. Our host greets us and explains what will happen over the course of the next few hours, scattering his introduction with camp innuendos at the expense of the attendees. These events are held every weekend at haunted venues up and down the country, and many here are regulars, equipped with high-tech instruments, ready to track down whatever hides in the night. As far as ghost hunting goes, Honour and I are rank amateurs.

We take up our torches and are led out into the auditorium. A room of quite staggering scale and beauty, with a capacity of up to 3,000 — greater, even, than that of London's Coliseum. It has some of the aura of that majestic space, with its sweep of balconies fanning out from the stage. A tunnel-vaulted ceiling rises in an arc overhead, decorated with plaster panels, each one individually composed of elaborate patterns. Eight boxes flank the stage, painted mauve with lime, pink and gold plasterwork. Above the proscenium arch, delicate and fading, a mural of seraphim and cherubim, larking about in the clouds.

Frank Matcham was the consulting architect here, and his influence may be seen in these ornate trimmings. The architects principally responsible for the building were Mangnall and Littlewood, who designed numerous buildings in the North of England, including Blackpool's Empress Ballroom. But this was their crowning glory. So proud were they of their creation that it seems their spirits refuse to leave — previous ghost hunters claim to have encountered the two architects in their office on the first floor.

How could one not be touched by the air of melancholy that hangs so thick over a setting like this? An empty auditorium is always a little uncanny; it seems bereft of purpose, echoing with the absent thunder of a thousand hands applauding. The Morecambe Winter Gardens Theatre is the trophy of another era, designed to accommodate great crowds of people, now left to rot in the unmoving darkness. No wonder ghosts might wish to take possession of it.

A cast of spirits makes its home here. A frustrated dancer who never achieved her dreams; a woman in RAF uniform, stranded from the time when the Air Force used the theatre as a training base. An audience member who fell to her death on the marble stairs, and the married lover she tussled with (whether she fell or was pushed is a secret held by the stones). Each, it seems, is unable to work their way free of the emotional grasp the theatre exerted on them during life, and so here they stay, run aground in the shadowy hinterland that lies beyond our ken.

Gazing up through the proscenium arch, I think of the weirdness that unfolds on a stage, the process by which whole casts of characters are invoked each night, attaining all their energy from the collective engagement of audience members and performers — our willingness to suspend disbelief — and then how they vanish, dissipating like mist burned off by the morning sun. During the brief, two-hour traffic of the stage, the theatre demands a duality of belief, a willingness to question the certainty of our own version of reality. What are we doing here, if not summoning up apparitions?

From somewhere beneath the stage comes a loud, insistent knocking. We all twitch and look around at each other nervously. But it's just the exhalations of an old building, rudely disturbed in its slumber.

We move on through the theatre. There are signs of revival — a new carpet laid in the dressing room, the sharp smell of fresh paint backstage. In 1986, the Friends of the Winter Gardens was formed, and volunteers began to clean and preserve the building. Now gigs and events are presented here from time to time, and they are hopeful about invigorating the site into new life. But the challenge is enormous, and the building itself seems to resist it, hunching inwards around its fading glamour. The shifting beams of our torches alight on indications of creeping dilapidation: puddles accumulating in unwatched corners; rusting metalwork thrusting through plaster curlicues, the bones of the building laid bare.

In the entrance hall, two marble staircases sweep upwards from an intricate mosaic floor. Climbing to the dress circle, I catch the pungent aroma of tobacco. Later I learn that this is a common phenomenon in this part of the theatre, which is said to be haunted by the ghosts of a cigarette seller and the caretaker who became obsessed with her.

It's time for the ghost hunt to begin. Beneath the stage in the trap room, we set up a series of torches and electromagnetic field monitors at various intervals across the floor. Then, we stand stock still in the dark, eyes and ears straining for the shadows and whispers that might indicate a spectral presence. The bolder in the group start calling out: "If you're here, show yourself. We mean you no disrespect". The only sound is the blood hammering in my ears.

A few moments pass, and then, suddenly, a torch switches itself on, a low shaft of light spreading out across a dusty arc of floor. A collective intake of breath. Cameron, a member of our party who claims to have psychic abilities, explains that he's picking up two presences in the room: the disappointed dancer and a darker presence — a man who was obsessively in love with her. "He's standing right behind you, looking over your shoulder," he tells one of the group, who deals with the news in a remarkably sanguine manner. "Can you make the torch switch off for us?" he asks, and, as if on command, we're plunged back into darkness.

"Is there a woman here you love? Someone you can't let go?" The electromagnetic field monitor begins blinking furiously on and off, and the excited ghost hunters gather around it, ask questions, encourage the spirit to step towards the device and light it up for yes, and to move away from it for no. The device flashes in response with persuasive accuracy.

One of the hosts, who has maintained the demeanour of a bored Saturday girl throughout these apparent manifestations, suggests we have a go at table-tilting. In the half-light, we put our fingertips on a table and summon the spirits to prove their presence by moving it. The table begins to rock back and forth violently with a febrile, almost sexual energy. A terrible growl echoes through the room. "That was my stomach, sorry," says Honour.

The whole thing has the atmosphere of a school trip, everyone giggly and excitable. I wonder what it is that motivates these people to give up their Friday night, and a not insubstantial wodge of cash, to spend time in the company of the undead. Does it fill a hole, as religion does, reassure them that this realm is only part of the picture? But it seems to be less profound than that; their manner suggests what they're here for is the adrenalin rush, as if this were little more than a sinister amusement park. They keep repeating their mantra, "we mean the spirits of this place no disrespect", but in fact they goad and tease them in the hope of stirring displays of prowess. At one moment, they begin whistling, 'winding up' the spirits by breaking a thespian taboo, and I feel, suddenly, defensive of this building and its ghosts.

Later, we gather around a 'ghost box', a device designed to pick up electronic voice phenomena, and try to make out words and phrases. "It told someone to fuck off, once," says our host, encouragingly.

Things turn nasty at 2 a.m. A group of us is up in the circle bar, near the old architects' office, doing a Ouija board. The glass is just flying around it, and as I touch it with the most glancing of contacts, it's hard to believe it can gain such momentum purely from the slight pressure of my finger. The spirit we're communing with initially purports to be the old theatre caretaker, then reveals he's the man whose lover died on the stairs nearby. "Did you kill your wife?" Cameron asks, and the glass almost tips over as it moves across the board towards the word YES. We glance around at each other. "Are you messing with us?" asks Cameron, and the glass whizzes over to YES again.

The ghost is encouraged to spell out its name, and it begins to do so, slowly and steadily: FREDERICK DEEMING. Cameron points out that this is the name of one of the men suspected of being Jack the Ripper. The spirit spells out DIE ALL and encourages us to FOLLOW ME TO HELL. A couple of us remove our fingers from the glass, gingerly, but three others press on, challenging the spirit that if it wants to frighten us, it must appear to us, and with my heart in my mouth I stare out into the swelling darkness of the room, hardly daring to breathe.

Nothing appears. The strange rocky landscape of

unidentifiable articles of furniture that might so readily attain a ghoulish character in the gloom are impassive. But it's all become too much; we make our excuses, and step out into the still, quiet night. As I take gulps of briny Morecambe air, I realise I've been holding my breath. Honour later confesses that through the last few minutes she was silently reciting the Lord's Prayer in her head, and I feel surprisingly glad she did so.

Wandering back to our hotel, we agree it's either the most sinister or the silliest way we've ever spent a Friday night. We can't be sure which. Certainly some of what we've experienced lies at the very outer limits of what I can rationalise. The flashing lights and the communion of the Ouija board have unsettled the logic of my senses.

One scientific explanation of the ghostly goings-on at séances is ideomotion, involuntary muscular actions caused by the subconscious of those gathered. If this is true then what the night in Morecambe seems to demonstrate is the power of the united imagination, how it can accrete until it becomes a physical force, something manifest that can cause tables to walk and glasses to hurtle. It's hard to resist parallels to the power of theatre and the beings we bring into shuddering, twitching life.

In the morning we shower and then stroll out along the

seafront, the night's demons blasted out by spoondrift. We stop at a bronze statue of the town's most famous son, the comedian Eric Morecambe, frozen in one of his familiar poses — one arm half raised, hand framing his grinning, bespectacled face, a foot aloft at a jaunty angle. For a few moments, we pause to take the obligatory snaps with him for our social media streams, jumping in the air, great gurns on our faces. Engraved in stone at his feet is one of his quotes: *All of life is based on timing.* I think of our night spent earnestly tipping tables, misattributing stomach rumbles, and how we leaned in, attempting to make voices of all that white noise.

Life is, after all, rather a grand joke, in which we are very often the punch line.

9

SHELLEY THEATRE

Boscombe, Dorset

A doctors' surgery. Vanity Fair. The poet's son. A lock of hair. A guitar. A heart in a silk-lined box.

I WALK TO THE SHELLEY THEATRE from Pokesdown station, up the stretch of coast at Boscombe, passing body boarders crashing about in spumy shallows, a volleyball rising in a luminous arc against the horizon. Then I turn up a path through woodland into a stretch of sun-dappled park. The banter of two teenagers playing a chaotic game of tennis unsteadies the hot afternoon.

The newly redeveloped Shelley Manor stands in front of me, facing out across lawns, a mismatched spread of building that looks like it was designed through a game of consequences. The original house that stood here, Boscombe Cottage, and its estate, was bought in 1849 by Percy Florence Shelley, the only surviving child of poet Percy Bysshe Shelley and writer Mary Shelley. He began a lavish programme of renovation with the intention that his ailing mother should eventually live here, but she died in 1851 from a suspected brain tumour before the work was complete. So Percy Florence and his wife, Jane, moved in instead, splitting their time between Boscombe and their London home in Chelsea's bohemian Tite Street.

Tragedy marks the Shelley family story. A macabre fascination with how Percy Bysshe Shelley's heart ended up in a silk-lined box at Shelley Manor has prompted my visit. I want to discover what role the theatre played in this strange narrative, so befitting of a house built for the author of *Frankenstein*.

The exterior of the building offers few clues to its history. The original part, the east wing, has recently been converted into a smart doctors' surgery with an apricot stuccoed façade. The west wing is a box-fresh extension containing 13 high spec flats overlooking the tennis court. In the centre is the theatre: a three-storey red-brick building with a pitched slate roof, five lunette windows above a row of double doors and, on the top floor, a large balcony.

To say Percy Florence was a theatre enthusiast would be an understatement — he liked the artform so much, he built three of his own. He had a theatre erected at his home in Chelsea, only ever used for private gatherings after a neighbour, worried about the noise, obtained a court order preventing it from opening to the public. At Shelley Manor, he initially built a temporary construction in the garden in around 1850, later replacing it with the current, permanent indoor theatre. The first performances were presented in 1866.

In the years since Percy Florence and Jane lived here, Shelley Manor has been through many incarnations. In 1911 it became a girls' school. During the Second World War it was requisitioned as a Home Guard and First Aid Centre. Later, it became an art and technical college, during which time the theatre was used as a canteen. The college closed in 1992 and the structure fell into disrepair: metal grates covered doorways; the windows were boarded up and graffitied; and for a time, the manor was squatted. Photos show the building damp and bruised, mouldering like a wind-fallen fruit on the overgrown lawns.

In 2005 the contract was awarded for the site's development into a medical practice; getting the theatre operational again was part of the deal, and it fitted with a forward-thinking notion that the proximity of a creative environment might be conducive to the good health of the surgery's patients. The building is a series of delightful disjunctures, as the exterior hints. I pass a gaggle of patients queuing in an egg-yolk-yellow waiting room. Then I move through a door and I'm suddenly in a trendy cocktail bar; gilt mirrors hang against chipboard, chandeliers clash with exposed breezeblocks — a rough, mismatched aesthetic that either points to the joint's hipster aspirations, or the fact that it isn't quite finished. In a corridor, someone is cutting a piece of MDF on a sawhorse.

A caricature of Percy Florence Shelley from an 1879 issue of *Vanity Fair* hangs on the wall. He is ruddy-cheeked, with an equine nose and a reddish beard, shoulders thrust back and hands buried deep in his pockets; a homburg hat balances on his head. The image is captioned 'The Poet's Son'. A perfunctory epithet; I wonder what life must have been like growing up in the shadow of two of English literature's most towering figures?

Percy Florence barely knew his father, who died when his son was two years old. Percy Bysshe Shelley had led a short and tumultuous life. Born in 1792 to a noble family, he was disowned by his father after being expelled from Oxford for publishing a pamphlet called *The Necessity of Atheism*, and had then eloped with a 16-year-old school girl named Harriet Westbrook. He met Mary Godwin, the daughter of political philosopher William Godwin and women's rights activist Mary Wollstonecraft, in 1812. In 1814 they began an affair, ran away together and spent the summer travelling through Europe. In 1816 they stayed at Lake Geneva with a group of friends including Lord Byron. It is there, during a late-night scary story contest, that Mary came up with the plot for her great novel *Frankenstein; Or, the Modern Prometheus*. Harriet killed herself that December; Mary and Percy Bysshe were married almost immediately.

Percy Florence was born in 1819, the only one of Percy Bysshe's children with Mary Shelley to survive past infancy. Two and a half years later, Percy Bysshe drowned off the coast of Italy, aged just 29. By the time he died, he had already produced a substantial body of work that distinguished him as one of the great Romantic poets. Mary never remarried, and dedicated the rest of her life to editing Percy Bysshe's poems, as well as pursuing her own literary projects; after *Frankenstein; Or, the Modern Prometheus*, her works included

Valperga: Or, the Life and Adventures of Castruccio, Prince of Lucca, *The Fortunes of Perkin Warbeck: A Romance* and *The Last Man*, as well as short stories, essays and travel writing.

From the cocktail bar, I step into the theatre. It is a high-ceilinged room, originally intended to accommodate 300; the floor is now covered with an MDF rake, holding 160 unusually comfortable seats donated by the local Imax cinema. At one end is a raised stage, lit by rows of LED lighting overhead. Peeling plaster and rough, exposed red brickwork give it a rather decrepit charm. It has seen better days, and many of the original features — such as the wooden stage machinery that Percy Florence built to operate the scenery — have been lost. But there are clues to its past glory: garland-patterned coving running around the proscenium arch; along one wall, double doors, swagged in red velvet. At the back of the auditorium, raised up high in the wall, is a window, half covered by a wooden shutter, where a projector is set up. This was Lady Shelley's bedroom. Towards the end of her life, when she was unwell, she would sit here and watch the action on the stage below.

In addition to staging plays, the theatre hosted balls and parties. I imagine the doors opening onto the park, the guests drifting towards the lawn, their laughter lifting on the balmy seaside air. Newspaper reports from the time attest to what an impressive dwelling this was. A journalist from *The Bournemouth Graphic* described 'a truly magnificent room ... The walls are panelled with bright floral designs in fresco on a very light ground, and the beautiful arched roof is painted a deep shade of blue. The stage is large, and equipped with every appliance for dramatic representations — wings, flies, traps and whatnot.' It is clear that, even in the context of extravagant lifestyles led by the affluent in Victorian society, this private theatre was something unusual. 'We conceive of few finer additions of this character to the private houses of the wealthy to be found throughout the country,' wrote *The Poole and South Western Herald* in 1866.

On this stage, Percy Florence mounted an extensive programme of amateur theatricals, to which he gave himself wholeheartedly — painting and decorating scenery, writing, composing and performing. Although much of the programme was presented to a private audience — with many notable guests drawn from their circle including Robert Louis Stevenson and Sir Henry Irving — they often opened their doors to the public, raising funds for local charitable causes. Percy Florence had a predilection for farce and an eye for a pun, and the bill included such fare as *A Comedy of Terrors*, *A Model of a Wife* and *A Pantomime Rehearsal*, which sounds rather like an early precursor of *The Play That Goes Wrong*.

It must have been tough to be the son of such an august

artistic lineage; to be ordinary in the wake of brilliance. Perhaps the theatre was where Percy Florence hoped to carve a niche of his own. The rewards of the form must have appealed — the immediate applause, unlike the restrained creep of a poem, which breathes long after it leaves its author's hand. And what a declaration of intent, to build a theatre of your own, already proposing — insisting upon — the meeting with your audience, the act of recognition that must inevitably follow.

His work seems to have delighted audiences well enough at the time: 'The acting of Sir Percy Shelley as Tim Dibbler was capital, particularly when he expresses his intention to be very calm, but in the next sentence breaks out into very ungentle tones,' wrote *The Poole and South-Western Herald* in its 1866 review of *Good for Nothing*.

After he drowned, Percy Bysshe's body was cremated on the beach near Viareggio. Lord Byron was present, as were Trelawny and Shelley's friend Leigh Hunt. Trelawny later recorded the event in his biography of the poets, *Recollections of the Last Days of Shelley and Byron*. He described, in visceral detail, the fire taking hold of the drowned poet, his body split open and his brains turned to ash. Lord Byron 'could not face this scene', and took off for a swim in the sea, asking Trelawny to preserve the skull; but, Trelawny wrote, 'remembering that he had formerly used one as a drinking cup, I was determined Shelley's be not so profaned'. His scruples did not extend to Shelley's heart, which, curiously, did not burn but remained in one piece. Trelawny was seized with a desire to save it, and plunging his hand into the blaze, plucked the heart out, burning himself badly in the process.

Trelawny handed the heart over to Hunt who, after some persuasion, passed it on to Mary Shelley. She wrapped it in a silk handkerchief, and apparently carried it about with her for years. When she died, Percy Florence and Jane claimed they found the remains of the heart in her desk, wrapped in the pages of Percy Bysshe's poem 'Adonais'.

It ended up here, on a floor now full of white fire doors with chrome plates bearing the names of doctors. At the top of the stairs, I pause at a high, domed ceiling, trimmed with gold stars and painted marbled shades of greige, like storm clouds reflected in a murky pond. Standing beneath it, I say a few words, and my voice rises and circles about overhead, as if it's not entirely my own.

This was the sanctum, the room to which they brought Shelley's heart. Inspired by their acquisition, the Boscombe Shelleys began to gather paraphernalia from the lives of Percy Bysshe, Mary and their contemporaries. In a room illuminated by red lamplight, they built their collection, including several locks of hair, Percy Bysshe's left glove and a damp-thickened copy of Sophocles that, it was claimed, the drowned poet held in his hand when he was found. On the wall hung a copy of Amelia Curran's portrait of him, pale-skinned and slender. What remained of the heart was transferred into a silk-lined box.

Lady Jane Shelley was the driving force behind the composition of this reliquary. Her friend Maud Rolleston later recalled being invited upstairs. 'She said "I want to show you my special relics, and you will know the spot then where I love to sit and where I spend all my time when I am alone."' It was a strategic exercise, part of the project to build the Shelley legend. But there was a strong spiritual aspect to these endeavours too; the Bodleian Libraries hold examples of Jane's automatic writing, as she tried to commune with Mary Shelley beyond the grave. They were attempting to invest this spot with ghosts that had never set foot here in life.

In the evening, I take up my cinema seat for the evening's show. The auditorium is perhaps a quarter full, mostly older punters, with a few families and a local group of students, sipping on cocktails from the bar. The play, almost inevitably, is inspired by *Frankenstein* — a puppetry show that is slightly lost on the large stage. In this version, the story focuses on an inventor who, mourning his wife, tries to find a way to revive her. The attempts fail, and the inventor discovers that he can't, after all, breathe life back into the dead, however hard he tries.

In 1885, an article appeared in *The Athenaeum* suggesting that the charred organ they kept here all that time wasn't actually Percy Bysshe's heart at all: it was his liver. The theory has some credence on the basis that the liver is the last organ to burn in a fire, particularly given it would have been swollen with seawater. Hunt and Trelawny, not being anatomists, may well have been mistaken in their identification of the organ. It's impossible to know. By the time Percy Florence died in 1889, the heart was little more than dust, and it was buried with him at St Peter's Church in Bournemouth. Mary Shelley had already been interred there after her death. In acquiescence to her wishes to be laid to rest with her parents, Mary Wollstonecraft and William Godwin's bodies had been exhumed from the graveyard of St Pancras Old Church in London and buried alongside her.

It's difficult to explain what it is that seems to me rather pitiful about the history of Shelley Manor. I'm probably ascribing it undue pathos; the Boscombe Shelleys had a charmed life, mounting performances to entertain their celebrity friends, filling the halls of their lavish home with art and with laughter. Plus, they were Victorians — a macabre fascination with the dead, dismembered body parts and all, was practically obligatory.

Still, there's something about the fudged history the

Shelleys cultivated here that strikes me as sad, as if their own presence wasn't enough to make the place vibrant. And of course, it wasn't; it's the spectre of Percy Bysshe and Mary that makes this ordinary theatre so fascinating and strange today. But theatre is not only about summoning ghosts; it is about slaying them. What matters is the narrative we are forging together in the present.

I think of Percy Florence standing on this stage. I hope he felt the space was his own; I hope that he was happy. *Man's yesterday may ne'er be like his morrow/Nought may endure but Mutability*. Perhaps, now and then, he took hold of the slippery moment: the heart that is a heart, and now is beating.

10

SUMMERHALL

Edinburgh

A swimming pool. A trampoline. A naked art student.
A colony of bees. Faust in a box.

EDINBURGH. IF YOU CAN LIVE INSIDE THEATRE, this is where the idea becomes manifest. For one month each year, the city is a stage. I mean this in a literal sense; in August 2017, there are 3,398 performances in settings including a football stadium, a swimming pool, a ladies' toilet, a canal barge, a shipping container, a flooded church — every lecture hall, disused shop or room above a pub reconceived as a theatre.

The topography of the city itself has been backdrop and muse in shows like Duncan Speakman's *As If It Were The Last Time*, an audio guided performance through the urban landscape that prompted participants to look at the world around them as if they'd never see it again, and David Leddy's *Susurrus*, which led audiences on a sonic adventure through the Royal Botanic Garden. This year, the British Council has commissioned *Imagine 2037*; eight artists, all migrants from across the world, have written instructions for an imaginary festival to be staged in 20 years' time at the top of Arthur's Seat — the extinct volcano that dominates the Edinburgh skyline. 'Looking down towards the city, trace the outline of the cityscape with your arm,' Maru Rojas writes, in *Six Actions for Transitioning*. 'Repeat at least 20 times, so the movement is committed to muscle memory. Mentally compare this memory to your visual memory of the city 20 years ago.'

Muscle memory. I know Edinburgh like this — by its cobbles, the ache in my calves, the way it tears my shoes apart.

I map it by the dash from show to show, venue to venue, Pleasance to Assembly to Zoo to Underbelly. I came here first in my late teens, and then in my early twenties, soon after I'd left drama school. By then I had a job at a theatre publicity agency. Each summer, we packed up our London office and headed north, taking over a flat in one of the huge Georgian buildings in New Town. For five weeks, we lived and worked together, gathering each day around a dining table strewn with half-eaten packets of biscuits and reviews ripped from *The Scotsman* and *The Guardian*, issuing press releases from our laptops and making calls to harangued arts editors. The usual parameters of working life didn't apply, there were no weekends, critics crashed on our sofa, we barely slept, we had ill-advised love affairs, we sang karaoke we regretted, we turned up at award ceremonies for the free bacon sandwiches, and we watched shows — so many of them — six or more a day sometimes, as if they were sustenance.

I fell in love with this city. The narrow alleyways and flights of steps disappearing into darkness between towering gothic buildings or breaking into sudden, unexpected panoramas. That castle, standing above it all, like something from the pages of a Mervyn Peake novel. The air carried a sweet biscuity smell that I couldn't attribute for years, until someone explained it was the scent of malted barley, gusting in from the breweries on the outskirts of town. One night in a bar I met an American photographer who had moved to the city, he claimed, because "it has the best light in the world". Do people leave their families, resettle halfway around the globe, in pursuit of light? Somehow, here, it was plausible.

The location is not an accident. When Rudolf Bing founded the Edinburgh Festival in 1947, he sought a city with the infrastructure capable of supporting his planned programme of activity, with an aspect likely to appeal to tourists. Harry Harvey Wood, then director of the British Council in Scotland, suggested Edinburgh — it was a perfect fit.

Bing was an Austrian-born opera impresario, a Jewish émigré who had come to Britain in 1934 to escape Nazism. He was working as General Manager at Glyndebourne when he founded the festival. He had lofty aspirations — he wished to 'provide a platform for the flowering of the human spirit' and saw the arts as a means of promoting harmony in the wake of the War. In that first year, artists and companies travelled across Europe to be in the Scottish capital. Highlights included performances from Sadler's Wells, La Compagnie Jouvet De Théâtre de l'Athénée, Paris's L'Orchestre Colonne. Bruno Walter, a German-born conductor who had spent the war in exile in the United States, was reunited with the Vienna Philharmonic Orchestra for a performance of Mahler's *Das Liede von der Erde*, with Kathleen Ferrier as soloist.

How liberating it must have been, after all the years of fighting, to meet those from across Europe through art, not violence. The festival anticipated the freer cultural era to come; a few years later, in 1963, art student Anna Kesselaar caused a scandal when she was wheeled naked across the balcony of the McEwan Hall during a drama conference, prompting the so called 'lady McChatterley' trial at which she was accused — and acquitted — of performing an indecent act in public. According to journalist Bernard Levin, the event marked the beginning of the late 20th century's more permissive society.

The festival was also responsible for a less racy, but nonetheless significant, evolution in British theatre, as the demand on Edinburgh's traditional performance spaces forced artists to think more laterally about where drama could happen. In 1953, Richard Burton and Claire Bloom starred in the Old Vic's production of *Hamlet* in the Church of Scotland's Assembly Hall. The auditorium was laid out in a thrust configuration, a mode of staging that had largely gone out of fashion in British theatre. Audiences were moved by the intimacy of witnessing these two great actors, just coming into the full force of their artistic potency, so close up, and were struck by their naturalistic performance style. As actor Robert Gillespie, who appeared in the production, commented to the BBC, "you could see modern theatre was groping its way to becoming something ... that was the seed that led to the classics being as popular as they are".

Worthy as its aspirations were, the Edinburgh Festival was also, at least in the early days, exclusive. Bing's predilection was for 'High Art'. The Glasgow Unity Theatre was an amateur group, part of a national arts movement with close ties to the communist party. They had had a runaway smash hit in 1946 with Robert McLeish's *The Gorbals Story*, which was performed over 600 times across the UK. The company wanted to be part of the first festival programme, but Bing refused. Glasgow Unity Theatre showed up anyway, performing Maxim Gorky's *The Lower Depths* — a bleak portrait of life in a Russian homeless shelter — as well as Robert Maclellan's *The Laird O' Torwatletie*. The fare was provocative, its defiantly working-class subject matter at odds with the 'bourgeois' content of Bing's programme. They were not the only group that turned up uninvited; seven other companies, wanting a piece of the action, took over venues across the city. So the Edinburgh Festival Fringe was born.

This spontaneous burst of creative activity seems characteristic of the spirit of the Edinburgh Fringe: always a celebration of the maverick spirit, where any performance that could happen, probably has — the more far out, the better. *Hamlet* on a bouncy castle, *Faust* in a box, shit-faced Shakespeare. Take any classic work, add a gimmick and you have the perfect recipe for a Fringe show. The constitution of the Edinburgh Festival Fringe Society, founded in 1958, states that it will take no part in vetting the festival's line-up. Anyone with an idea — with a dream — can be part of it; although the reality is that the expense of the enterprise is a barrier for many. I'm still moved, though, by the simplicity of that principle. I think the most beautiful thing at this festival is the way curious, fragile things that wouldn't work anywhere else are able to bloom.

I approach across The Meadows, a stretch of public parkland to the south of the city. Summerhall is ahead of me, glimpsed through the trees; it takes up an entire block, an early 20th-century construction in pinkish brown sandstone. Flat roofed, it is two-and-a-bit storeys of enormous casement windows, reflecting back a sky of fluffy white clouds. A grand frontage; but in spite of its classical flourishes — the pediments at both ends of the building, and the pillars holding a high arch over the main doors — it has rather an austere appearance. It isn't entirely complete — the story is that there were plans for a series of animal sculptures to adorn the front, but by the time the building work was finished in 1914, the stonemasons due to create them had been called up to the War, leaving it with this somewhat plain appearance. An incongruous tower, built in the late 1960s, stands at one end, connected by a glass walkway to the main building.

The windows are a clue to its past. At the start of the 20th century, the Dick Veterinary College acquired this site where a brewery had been. They began work in 1913 on the construction of a purpose-built veterinary college, following a design by architect David McArthy. The previous location, on Clyde Street, had been considered dark and dingy, an inadequate setting for the fiddly work of cutting up frogs and mice, so part of the brief here was to provide as much natural light as possible. Not everyone has been enthusiastic about the design of this building. The entry in 1984's *Buildings of Scotland* reads: 'Fag-end Wrenaissance ... the front a dreary frame of columns and pediments. Inside, the pompous stairhall is an epitome of bourgeois smugness.'

I wonder what the author would have made of it today. Outside, a shipping container bears on its roof a headless mannequin and a sign reading 'SÉANCE'. Tucked away around a corner, I spot a 'HIDDEN MARGARITA BAR' — the concealment somewhat compromised by its gold, holographic frontage. A row of bikes chained to a railing. One enthusiastic, early morning flyerer stands in the entrance and offers me a leaflet advertising a puppetry show.

I go through to the courtyard and sit down at a table covered with a film of grease and cigarette ash from last night, and sip my takeaway coffee. Once used for exercising the animals, the courtyard is filled with makeshift awnings, a wooden shack selling beers and a gin van. A huge incinerator chimney rises into the sky — a flotsam of publicity posters has accumulated around its base. The Summerhall staff all look hungover, unready for the day to begin, but they chat animatedly about the events of last night. "I'd like to do front of house at Adelaide and Prague fringes too," one of them says, as if this suspended reality could become a way of life.

I was here in 2011, the year Summerhall opened, for Action Hero's *Watch Me Fall*, a 'homemade stunt show' in the Dissection Room upstairs. The building had been a veterinary college until so recently that the performance was surrounded by specimens, unidentifiable creatures pickled in jars. "That year was amazing — you felt like at any point you might wake and the vets would be back saying what the hell are you doing," Verity Leigh, Summerhall's programme manager, tells me. It was the test run, and it proved a success. So Robert McDowell, a well-heeled economist with an artistic background — he studied art at the Slade and once worked as an assistant to Joseph Beuys — purchased the building, and turned it into what now lays claim to being Edinburgh's biggest arts venue.

The logistics of this building are dizzying. The team runs a year-round programme of performance, but during the fringe its output swells: 250 staff work here each summer to present 100 shows, Leigh tells me, packed into six main performance spaces, as well as oddball nooks and crannies around the venue. "We don't ever tell people we have theatres, just these performance spaces, and each of them is very different and has its own feel and aesthetic," Sam Gough, Summerhall's general manager, says. "No dressing rooms, no backstage passes, no flytowers, no pass throughs."

When I've finished my coffee, I go for a wander. The War Memorial Library houses *Early Events: Five Narrative Sculptures*, an exhibition by Liliane Lijn. I note sand, the sound of the sea and the smell of lavender. I pass a room where somebody is playing the drums and a 'sensory play for early years and their grown ups'. 130 businesses have their base here now, and there is a brewery on site once more. A colony of two million bees lives on the roof.

Upstairs, the rooms are empty; no one is about. From a window I can see Arthur's Seat in the distance, brown-stained and craggy, tiny black figures on its face leaning forwards into the climb. I have the sense that this building is still becoming itself, stranded between its identities as a scientific institute and an arts venue. Perhaps I imagine the smell of formaldehyde, but locked doors carry signs reading *Cage Store* and *Compressed Gas*; one bears a directive to 'MAKE SURE INNER DOOR IS CLOSED BEFORE OPENING'. The Summerhall team rather likes this disjuncture. "The rooms have completely different atmospheres — the Demonstration Room, for instance, can feel quite creepy, like someone's recently killed a horse in there," Leigh says. "We like work that's got a scientific or animal theme — it's always got to be the right show". A room in the basement has been transformed into a beach for a performance, the floor covered with sand, rows of orange deck chairs awaiting an audience. In the corner, an old metalworking lathe gathers dust.

Back downstairs, I join the queue for the show I'm here to see. I bump into a director I know — in Edinburgh, I'm always bumping into people I know, or half recognise. Yesterday, in a queue for a show at the Pleasance, I got chatting to a guy who, after years in the music industry, is trying to break into theatre. I gave him some sage words of advice. "It's important to get a good Twitter following. And remember, always make your show 10 minutes shorter," I said. Turns out it was the lead singer of rock band The Feeling.

We file into the Anatomy Lecture Theatre, a horse-shoe of 58 flip-up seats arranged in a steep rake beneath a mucky, vaulted skylight, obscured with black tarpaulin. Pale blue paintwork of a vaguely institutional hue adorns the walls; up front, there is a smudged blackboard and an old basin. The first row of seats is raised to eye level behind a wooden barrier, allowing a clear view of the action, and, I assume, protecting onlookers from errant splatters of blood. Today, in the centre, a woman is bouncing on a trampoline. Beside her, another woman is doing a jigsaw puzzle. The first woman can't get off the trampoline. The second woman begrudgingly tries to help her.

The Anatomy Lecture Theatre is the oldest surviving veterinary college lecture theatre of its type in the United Kingdom. Once animals were dissected here, but now it is a performing arts venue like any other nook or cranny of Edinburgh at this time of year.

As thrilling as the idea of this annual transmutation of the city into one epic arts venue is, I can't pretend the reality is not exhausting, no doubt particularly so for the people who live here. 'Edinburgh' comes to mean 'festival', a metonym for late nights and discarded flyers and so much culture, so thick you get swallowed by it. When I arrived a couple of days ago, my taxi driver told me, "every year I promise myself I'll go to a show, and I never do". We bitched about the traffic and the busy-ness and the stupid tourists who never look where they're going. "So you live here, do you?" he asked. I admitted that I didn't and the conversation fell quiet.

But for me at least, returning each summer has been a necessary grounding, a reminder of what it's all for. After the show, I am queuing up to use a toilet. I spot a grotty mattress leaning against a wall. 'This is a prop, do not move' reads a handwritten sign. Who does it belong to? Where did they get it? How did they bring it here? And for a moment I find myself imagining how someone would have loaded it up in a van with the rest of their props and set off to Edinburgh, practicing their lines as they went, stopping off at the services for coffee and boiled sweets, their hopeful cargo stored in the back.

What a fine thing, to be in possession of a mattress that might, like a magic carpet, lift you.

11

THE THEATRE OF SMALL CONVENIENCE

Great Malvern, Worcestershire

A hospital issue bedpan. A child's painting of a cat.
A miniature skull. The Hale-Bopp. Insurance bills.
A fever dream.

I ARRIVE IN GREAT MALVERN straight from a week at the Edinburgh Festival Fringe — overexposed to a jam-packed schedule of shows, sleep deprived, something unsettling lurking in my gut.

The Malverns are some contrast. I take the London Midland to Birmingham and then, after a 20-minute wait, a two-carriage train that chugs its way through the countryside. I'm the only person to disembark on an empty platform bathed in late summer sun. Walking up a residential street of Victorian villas, I pass a woman in a dressing gown who is clutching a hospital issue cardboard bedpan. In a ribbon-trimmed VW beetle outside a church, a girl in a wedding dress sits beside her father, waiting.

In Great Malvern, the hills make their presence felt. They fill the sky behind the town, their pressing greenness freshening the air. They are evidence of the fact that this is a watery setting, with over 60 springs and wells ranged across the local landscape. The Malverns are said to have restorative powers, giving rise to the area's popularity as a centre for hydrotherapy in the Victorian era. While the waters failed to cure serious illnesses — Charles Darwin's 10-year-old daughter, Anne, died here of suspected tuberculosis in spite of receiving 'water cure' treatment — shops like Aquarius New Age on the High Street attest to the Malverns' continuing mystical allure. The residents are "poshos and hippies", my friend, whose parents have recently moved here, tells me later.

In the 1930s George Bernard Shaw spent each August walking in the hills and swimming in spring-fed pools that have long since become overgrown or inaccessible. Several of Shaw's plays premiered at the Festival Theatre, still a thriving cultural hub in the town centre, now with an additional performance space, cinema and restaurant. Edward Elgar also found inspiration here, composing in his head as he strode across the verdant contours of his home county. 'There is music in the air, music all around us,' he wrote. 'You simply take as much as you require.'

It's fitting, in a town where culture and water are so intimately linked, that a theatre should be situated in a former WC. The Theatre of Small Convenience is housed in a Victorian gents' toilet constructed from purply-grey Malvern stone. Outside, a bright blue sign announces its name. Ornately decorated tiles cover one wall — a handprint, a Union Jack, a child's painting of a cat. Strange stone faces with blank eyes press out of the thin bank of vegetation that runs around the theatre's edge.

In front of the theatre is a giant, freestanding puppet: William Shakespeare, as if imagined by the *Spitting Image* team, carved in wood and costumed in an ornate attire of lace, hand-painted gold and blue. A pair of sunglasses balances precariously on his nose, guarding against the midday glare.

His midriff has, with little ceremony, been unbuttoned, and inside is a tiny stage — peopled with a cast including a bear, a horse, and a plastic, Ken doll Hamlet (complete with miniature skull). All about the person of this curious figure passersby have attached small white labels, scribbled with lines from Shakespeare: 'I'm better than you are — I'm a fool and you're nothing'; 'One man in his time plays many parts'; 'We are such stuff as dreams are made on.'

A sign nearby proclaims: 'This tiny building houses the smallest theatre (building) in the world, as featured in the *Guinness Book of Records 2002*. Transformed from an old Victorian Gentleman's lavatory, Dennis Neale founded the theatre, which opened, with the help of a committee, in November 1999.

Since its opening, besides being the venue for Dennis's quirky puppet shows, it has had performances, both professional and amateur, of drama, poetry, storytelling, music and monologues, and even a day of opera!'

Neale comes out to greet me. Dressed in a black polo neck, he has sharp blue eyes, a pointed beard and silver hair curling down over his shoulders. Later I'll take a photo of him grinning beside his figurine of the Bard; the resemblance is striking.

Everything about this theatre is a tribute to his invention. In the 10-square-metres space, Neale has constructed a sound system from the innards of a piano and an industrial spring he pulled out of a skip. A dismembered double bass has transformed into a flamingo, complete with feather boa plumage. At the back is an old church pew for the audience to sit on — "the dress circle" — and a huge horn-shaped amplifier hangs overhead. "I use it to stop people nodding off," he says.

Neale took over the building in March 1997. Prior to his acquisition, and after it had gone out of service as a toilet, it had served as a children's clothes store. Later, it was a junk shop, where he would pick up bits and pieces for the puppets he was experimenting with creating. When the proprietor told him it was due to close, Neale commented in passing that the building "would make a wonderful miniature theatre".

"I don't know why really, I'd never been on the stage, never had anything to do with acting. I just had this idea off the top of my head." Three weeks later, having negotiated a peppercorn rent with the council, he was in.

It was, he points out, the month of the Hale-Bopp — the record-breaking comet that brought on a kind of international hysteria, causing internet users to pore over conspiracy theories, and the Heaven's Gate cult to commit suicide en masse, believing they would be teleported to a spaceship travelling in the comet's wake. In a season when surreal ideas seemed legitimate, the story of The Theatre of Small Convenience delighted the media, combining as it did two of Britain's favourite things — Shakespeare and toilet humour. Editors found it irresistible, and headlines appeared in the tabloid press: 'To Pee or Not To Pee', 'Shakespeare in Lav', 'As Loo Like It'. It took two years of hard work to raise the funds to transform the space. The theatre eventually opened its doors to the public in 1999.

Neale invites me to take a seat in front of the tiny stage. It calls to mind the ornamentation of a Matcham theatre but on a minute scale; fashioned from dismembered furniture parts, painted gold or copper plated. The proscenium arch is an old tea tray. Neale has a magpie-like eye for this stuff, bric-a-brac purchased for a few pence, drawn from other people's detritus and lent new beauty by their presence here. Everything seems to have its position in the order of the Theatre of Small Convenience, intricate and precise as a clock. He describes the theatre as a spider's web — it's impossible to walk past without getting caught up in it. He performs his repertoire of miniature shows up to 22 times on a Saturday, for a maximum audience of 12, on demand as people drop by.

On the door is a gallery of dog-eared photographs of past performances in action. A pair of performers in *Beano*-style papier-mâché masks, engaged in some kind of scientific experiment. A nine-piece opera ensemble, heads lifted, giving full voice to their song. The opera, he tells me, was two hours long; halfway through, there was a break, and everyone went to the pub up the road for a pint before the show resumed. There have been other performances — *The Pied Piper* from an artist who makes and sells recorders all over Europe, work from a local playwright, a show addressing LGBTQI+ issues. "Some actors haven't been prepared. They say — where's the dressing room? But if you have a sense of fun, a sense of adventure, it's a great place."

For the most part, though, Neale mounts his own plays, works as diminutive as the venue. Each is just 10 minutes long, with titles like *Princess Spoil Tart and the Planet Marzipan* — set on a planet where the inhabitants only eat sweets. Today's show is *Unsuitable Acts for the Stage: Quackery Codswallop* — a brief, absurdist satire on the arts with dramatis personae include 'Sean the Shy Singer', 'Titus the Too Tall Dancer', 'The Queen of Arts', and an underwater opera singer who warbles waterily. A stray eyeball leers around at the audience on a concertina camera lens; a sailor sets sail in a boat built from broken violin parts, accompanied by a nonsense narrative worthy of Edward Lear: "Captain Stradi, on various voyages, sets off from the nearest shore. A violin storm, that's not the norm, I mustn't crescendo the score!"

Neale didn't engage with theatre much in his early life; as a child, his parents didn't take him, and later, although he was creative, he was put off by the expense. "It's a minority sport, you'd have to admit that, wouldn't you?" he says. He describes a life of "continuous poverty", a series of jobs that never resolved into a career, working in factories and doing woodland surveillance in Wales, as a social worker, a trading weights and measures inspector.

It was surrealism that got under his skin. He cites Max Ernst as a significant influence. Ernst was a Dadaist artist who rejected rational, narrative-based form and instead mined his subconscious for inspiration, creating bright, disturbing images with names like *Here Everything is Still Floating* and *Two Children Are Threatened by a Nightingale*, snapshots from a fever dream.

A pivotal moment came when Neale stumbled into a show by Lit Moon Theatre "because it was free" and his kids wanted to go. He describes the scene with a precision that indicates how the performance etched itself on his psyche.

"There was a big white sheet and an audience. It was a shadow show — using live flame and torches. A man was standing by with a fire extinguisher ... it was so lovely — the flickering light ... there was an operatic singer and she didn't sing any words, just sound effects, and the magic, all the lights, I thought, this is fantastic." After that, he began experimenting with making puppets of his own.

There have been setbacks along the way. A few years ago, Neale developed throat cancer, and his voice wears a little thin as we speak. And the more mundane stuff, which nonetheless can be crippling: a leaky roof, for instance, and then the theft of the lead used to fix it. The current show got its name after Neale's work was repeatedly rejected for Arts Council funding. "I thought, 'who decides what's suitable?' So I did this show, *Unsuitable Acts for the Stage*." A witty response to an experience that may have made many others quit.

What is it that situates a person like this outside the system? In spite of its oddball nature, the benefits of the Theatre of Small Convenience to the local ecology are manifold. Tickets cost just £3, and Neale talks passionately about how important it is to him to keep it cheap and available, an idea that is, unlike for many theatre executives, rooted in personal experience — he "doesn't live in the realm" where he can afford to pay £25 for a ticket to a show, and he's passionate in his belief that no one should have to.

His theatre has become one of the top-rated tourist attractions in Great Malvern, punching well above its weight in terms of its significance to the local economy. And isn't it obvious that the general wellbeing of local residents must be greater for knowing they live in a town with a theatre in a Victorian Gents' toilet nearby? I hope it makes them smile a little more readily.

And yet, public subsidy has mostly eluded him. What Dennis lacks is the neat patois of the subsidised arts sector —

he doesn't talk about the theatre in terms of 'artistic excellence' or make 'the creative case for diversity'. This is an initiative born of a conviction that is entirely personal; impossible to reproduce — and it is this that bears it up. Enthusiasm, after all, is infectious.

"Sometimes naivety is a good thing. Perhaps an experienced person wouldn't have taken on such an enterprise."

He talks about the theatre as if he started it in spite of himself. "It was a once in a lifetime opportunity," he says. People like Dennis are the 'outsider artists' of theatre, I think: self-taught, operating at a remove from the institutes and frameworks that shape a sector. And it is this that makes their practice so distinctive. I'm reminded of an exhibition of outsider art I saw at the Hayward Gallery in 2013. In his *Guardian* review of the show, Adrian Searle wrote, 'none of what they have done feels like an alternative or a choice'. Many of the artists displayed were preoccupied with creating their own 'worlds' — from Bodys Isek Kingelez's cardboard models of fantastic, gravity-defying cities in fairground hues to A.G. Rizzoli's architectural renderings of imaginary buildings that doubled as symbolic portraits of people he knew.

A theatre, too, is a kind of world over which you may have dominion. But a dominion of the most benign kind, where you may experiment with ways of living, interact with different modes of being — before the lights come up in the auditorium, the curtains fall, the stage is swept and everyone goes to the pub for a pint to talk about what's happened.

When I go to leave, Neale points at a laminated scrap of paper stuck to his sign. 'Please note: we do not claim to be the smallest theatre in the world anymore. There is a tiny theatre in Germany what's in a bus shelter.'

"We're not actually the smallest theatre anymore," he explains, sadly. "But the sign cost so much to print."

Word will reach me, later, that the theatre is to close if a new owner can't be found. Evidently Neale makes no money from this enterprise, and he has never expected to; it's an irrational act of love, one destined, it seems, to be brought to an end by the most crushing of banalities — insurance bills. That we lose places like this is perhaps just the way of things. It is the very obtuseness of the Theatre of Small Convenience, the way it seems to sit at right angles with all logic, that is its gift, and yet when I hear the news it comes like a fist in my heart, because this is a place of sustenance, a reminder that following your own course is something to be celebrated.

Neale, I suspect, would be more sanguine. His reserves of childlike curiosity with the creative potential in the world seem undepletable.

"Anyway, I'm working on a new theatre. One audience member — tiny puppets. The theatre fits over their head."

He's suddenly ablaze with the possibility of his new invention, fired with an energy that belies his age and health. "That really will be the smallest theatre in the world," he tells me, with a smile.

12

MULL THEATRE

Isle of Mull

The Cuban Missile Crisis. Newborn lambs. Chocolate cakes. A plate of chips. An t-Eilean Muileach. Love alters not.

I'M ESCAPING TO AN ISLAND. On the top deck of the Calmac Ferry from Oban, American tourists in expensive, padded jackets are looking through the viewfinders on their cameras, pointing at the landmarks sliding slowly into our wake. A high-pitched German tour guide tells a group of students about the rhododendron season; two women crack open a wild 10 a.m. bottle of wine, dangling their glasses over the crashing spume 20 metres below. I lean back in my seat, sip from a cup of scolding coffee, trying to keep the nausea of the 5.20 a.m. start from Glasgow at bay. It takes over three hours to get to the ferry port at Oban, a lovely train ride past lochs and mountains and lazy pink mists. I snoozed through all of it.

Now the morning is full of itself, a sky of bright, high clouds reflected on the metallic surface of the Sound of Mull. Everything is vast and faraway and beautiful. Craggy promontories stretch into the water, and in the distance is an ascending ridge of mountains, eddied with shadow, a dark mohawk of fir trees along its lowest reaches. On a headland, a castle is propped up with scaffolding, at risk of collapsing, returning to the crumbled heap of granite from which it emerged. I try to take it all in. But it is all so much bigger than I could possibly contain: a landscape indifferent to my gaze.

'Anyone who lives on an island will, sooner or later, come face to face with themselves,' wrote Barrie Hesketh, who, with his wife Marianne, founded the Mull Little Theatre. I am riding in the slipstream of the journey they took in 1963, one rainy August afternoon, when they loaded up a boat with whatever furniture they could and, with their three young sons, set sail for a new life on Mull.

The Heskeths — both professional actors who met and fell in love at the Central School of Speech and Drama — had been living in Edinburgh, where Barrie was a Drama Adviser to the Scottish Community Drama Association. His job took him all over Scotland, including, on several occasions, to Mull. "I remember standing on the deck of the boat on the way out," he later said. "I was watching the mast gently, gently rotating. I thought — this is where I want to be."

1963 was the height of the Cold War, when the recent international brinkmanship around the Cuban Missile Crisis led many to consider a new life beyond the range of the split atom. The Heskeths were old enough to remember the devastation caused by the bombs at Hiroshima and Nagasaki, and they wished to escape the central industrial belt of Scotland, where warships and submarines gathered on the River Clyde. So the couple took a leap into the unknown, using an unexpected inheritance to buy a family home in a tiny village at the heart of Mull.

They were beguiled by the romance of the escape to the island too. The Heskeths were true optimists who forged a life of adventure, rarely letting practical considerations get in the way of pursuing their idealistic visions. Early in their marriage they had bought a boat to live on. They had no idea how to sail. On board for the first time, there was a petrol leak, and it exploded — only as they swam away from the burning hull did they recall that they'd failed to insure it. Now they came to the island without a car and a less-than-robust plan for how they'd finance their new life. But once they'd dreamt up the idea, it became inevitable. Barrie later describes himself as being "wrapped in coils of enchantment".

What is it about islands that holds such sway over the imagination? Islands contain a contradiction — they suggest both the threat of isolation and the fantasy of escape. In countless fictional worlds, like those of *The Tempest*, *The Wicker Man* and *The Lord of the Flies*, island communities have been presented as microcosms of society, magnifying the best and worst of human nature. The island provides a perfect setting for drama — a sphere where personal narratives are amplified and politics played out at a human scale. In the theatre, the island becomes a mystical zone, 'full of noises, sounds, and sweet airs that delight and hurt not'. Perhaps theatre sees something of itself in the island too, a constrained site of human contact, bound by a wide, indifferent sea.

Mull's miniature capital Tobermory (population: 1,000)

comprises a harbour ringed with brightly painted houses, familiar to millennials and their parents as the fictionalised town of Ballamory in the early noughties children's TV show of the same name. The Mull Theatre is a couple of miles from the town centre. It's possible to wander up to it by a footpath that meanders through Aros Park, a stretch of forest full of ferns and rhododendrons overlooking the uninhabited Calve Island.

Located on the edge of the woodland, the theatre is an austere blue-black edifice clad in corrugated cement sheeting, reminiscent of the barns and outbuildings scattered across Mull. The building is constructed in two sections that don't quite align, chunky dark wedges whose roofs angle up towards one another. The plain façade is interrupted with windows of various sizes framed in heritage green. A modest set of double doors marks the entrance.

A practical building constructed on a budget, this is a work-in-progress, built in phases as money allows. In time it will spread outwards, with the addition of a cedar clad rehearsal space and workshops, and a wrap-around, glass-fronted foyer/bar with views across fields to Ben Hiant, a mountain on the Ardnamurchan peninsula.

Standing outside, the stillness is unnerving. I pull out my phone and record it so I can play it back when I'm once again sequestered in the cacophony of the city. The air is crowded with swallows, who chip-chip-chip and crepppp and urgh, underscored with the low bass note of a cuckoo. In the field opposite is a herd of sheep and their tiny, days-old lambs. It's that time of year, everything brand new, swelling with potential. Earlier, walking with friends by Loch Buie, I saw a ewe giving birth a few metres from the pathway, watched her strain as a profusion of tangled bloody limbs made its way from inside her, until, perhaps unglad of an audience, she crested a hill and disappeared into the distance.

The theatre wasn't always here. The Mull Little Theatre, as it was then known, was first established in Dervaig, a small village at the tip of Loch Cuin on the north coast of the island. Just seven miles from Tobermory, it can only be reached — even now — down a twisting, single-track road. Druimard, the Heskeths' new home, was in the village's former manse, the home provided for the local Free Church of Scotland minister. It's an astonishingly beautiful location — as almost everywhere on the island is — with sweeping views of dry moorland, brushstrokes of midnight green fir trees in the distance and, in the glen below, the shallow folds of River Bellart.

The Heskeths' new life wasn't all plain-sailing. They faced financial difficulties, blocked pipes and errant sheep. Yet what seems to have bonded Barrie and Marianne more than anything was an unquenchable hunger for life; a gung-ho spirit of adventure that sometimes verged on the foolhardy. In the end, it was naïve optimism that sustained them, each new challenge presenting an opportunity to test their creativity, and they rose to the occasion admirably, from using divining rods to fix a leak to setting up as a bed and breakfast to make ends meet.

The theatrical inclination, it seems, is one that's difficult to shake off. In the grounds of Druimard stood an old cow byre. Alone in the house one day, the Heskeths were wandering from room to room, thinking about new ways to subsist. "We both, more or less, realised it at the same time," Barrie commented. "We looked across at the little broken-down building and saw a theatre. We both said at once 'let's give it a try' without knowing exactly what we were going to do." A pleasing account of events that reminds me of the irresistible draw felt by Neale at the Theatre of Small Convenience towards his former gentlemen's lavatories. Perhaps potential theatres have their own gravitational force; they are just waiting for people of the right substance to pass into their orbit.

In the tumbledown structure, they built a miniature, 42-seat theatre, with a 14-by-10-foot stage. The whole project had a *Blue Peter* quality to it; theatre dimmers were created out of discarded preserve jars filled with brine, and Barrie crafted the seating from old beds from the guesthouse, bent into six crude settees. A rostrum was constructed from an upturned shop counter. The village amateur dramatic group donated a set of curtains, which they hung from the back of the stage, and a local cinema gave them some tip-up seating they no longer needed.

From then on, paying guests of the Heskeths enjoyed bed, breakfast and a show. Swiftly, the popularity of the enterprise grew, with audiences drawn from across the island and further afield; the auditorium was often filled with many more than its official capacity.

In this sequestered domain, far removed from the mainstream theatre and television that had defined their careers on the mainland, the Heskeths discovered a new kind of artistic freedom. They became masters of invention — liberated, paradoxically, by the constraints of the space and the resources available to them. The cast was just the two of them, but with puppets crafted from socks and the ingenious deployment of a Grundy tape recorder concealed in the set, they presented works with *dramatis personae* of dozens. The fare ranged from adaptations of Chekov and Wilde to their own experimental Punch and Judy shows, parodying world affairs; the audience would munch happily on the chocolate cakes that became the theatre's trademark.

Each evening would begin with Barrie, not yet in character, taking to the stage to welcome his audience, telling stories from the day, what their sons had been getting up to. A way of beating the bounds of the realm audience and performers would share. Then, slipping into costume and donning the mask of his character, the show would begin.

Eventually, the Heskeths stopped offering lodgings altogether to focus on their productions. For some time, the theatre was in the *Guinness Book of Records* as the smallest professional theatre in the UK. The summer season ran each year from April until September, and the company began to receive funding and to tour all over Europe. Other actors joined the company. One of them was Alasdair McCrone, who arrived as a recently graduated actor and went on to become the company's director from 1995.

Reading Barrie's utterly joyous book about those years, *Taking Off*, I'm left more than anything with a sense that the ramshackle theatre he and his wife created was a manifestation of the love they shared, as if it demanded all the possible worlds a theatre can conjure to contain it. Indeed, the first show they ever staged was *Two by Two*, a bill of short, light-hearted pieces from classical literature exploring love and marriage. Perhaps, through the words of Shakespeare, D.H. Lawrence, and George Bernard Shaw, they approached an expression of how they felt for each other.

How was the arrival of these thespians greeted? This was still an impoverished crofting community; it had never fully recovered from the devastating impact of the clearances of the 19th century, when significant numbers of islanders were violently removed from their homes by wealthy landowners to make way for new agricultural practices. So the presence, suddenly, of outsiders, with RP accents and extravagant puppets, in this tiny village of 100 people was treated by some with suspicion.

In 1981 a BBC crew visited to film a documentary about the Mull Little Theatre for *Arena*. In the local pub, one elderly resident voiced her reservations. "When people come into a place they would be expected to adopt a little of the ways of the place," she commented. "And if they don't do this the danger is that they're bringing in the culture that they came away from in the first place, and of course if it is a bigger culture than the island culture then I suppose the bigger culture takes over eventually."

It is a justifiable fear. The arts can provide a locale with its sense of self, a fact cynically drawn on by property developers and town planners to 'regenerate' areas — which is a way of saying, to change them. But for anyone who had visited the theatre, it must have been hard to read anything sinister into the Heskeths' enterprise — held together with PVA glue and sticky back plastic and a hefty personal overdraft. The theatre was run with a spirit of generosity that perhaps only an organisation built so clearly on personal passion can be;

audience members who found themselves unable to pay for tickets were often let in for free, and nearby campers washed out by island storms were allowed to kip on the stage.

In time, the theatre was adopted by the islanders, and even became a part of island identity. McCrone tells a story about the pupils of Dervaig primary school regularly being brought up to the theatre to watch shows. Asking their teacher what they had made of a particular play, he was told they weren't too sure about it. "Mind you," said the teacher, "they are quite hard to please. They see a lot of theatre."

McCrone says, "here we are in the middle of nowhere, you look out of the window of that school on to the sea and a bog and there's not much else, but the kids there see a lot of theatre. OK, we're doing our job."

The show is due to begin at 7 p.m. From 6.30 p.m. cars start arriving in the gravel car park, audience members ambling up across the lawn in the honeyed late afternoon sun. At a picnic bench, McCrone is eating fish and chips with his wife; their daughter kicks about a beaten-up football with their Welsh border collie nearby. People are chatting, helping themselves to Tunnocks teacakes from a trestle table underneath a marquee, dropping a few coins into the honesty plate.

The theatre moved here in 2008. The lease had expired on the Dervaig property and it was no longer fit for purpose

— the small stage, while charming, demanded significant compromises to the kinds of shows that could be presented, limiting the ambition of what had, by then, become one of the leading lights of Scotland's rural touring scene. It was also an attempt to shift the narrative around the theatre. Much of the appeal of the Mull Little Theatre resided in its quirkiness, and commentary in the media often expressed surprise that decent professional theatre should be produced in such an offbeat location, far removed from the bright lights of Glasgow or Edinburgh. But this account reinforced a stereotype that is troublesome to islanders — the idea that they are parochial, capable neither of producing nor of appreciating high quality art.[1]

The last words you would choose to describe the new building are 'quirky' or, indeed, 'charming'. It is, above all, somewhere designed for production; the architectural resonance with the farm buildings of Mull positions the theatre as a cottage industry and is in tune with the self-perception of many islanders. This is a site where work gets done.

---

[1] The old Little Theatre is now a boutique holiday home for two, available for hire through Isle of Mull Holiday Cottages, complete with wood burning stove, roll top bath, and tasteful nods to its theatrical heritage — a dressing room mirror trimmed with light bulbs, and a row of tip-up seating in the kitchen.

It was not only the building that changed; the 'Little' was also unceremoniously cut loose from the organisation's title. In fact, the building is referred to as a 'production centre' rather than a theatre, reflecting its emphasis on creating work for touring around the country, particularly to remote areas. A map of locations the company has visited is marked with a rash of red spots across the highlands and islands.

Over the years, they've performed on pretty much every island they possibly could, setting off in their van on the ferries that serve the Hebrides archipelago, pitching up in community centres and village halls, wherever they're invited to play. The best moments have been in the destinations where everyone has come out, 80-year-olds and 8-year-olds together, sticking about after the show to chat and share a plate of chips with the cast.

A few years after the move, in April 2013, Mull Theatre merged with An Tobar, the island's exhibition and gigs venue. It made sense in a context of increasing pressure on public subsidy to form a single entity that would be simpler for Creative Scotland to fund. Comar, meaning 'confluence' in Gaelic, was the name of the new organisation, complete with a brand-new board — many of whom were based on the mainland and had never lived on the island. But by November 2014, it was clear that Comar would not receive funding at the level required to operate as hoped. The following summer the board proposed a new management structure; as part of cost-cutting measures, McCrone and longstanding music director of An Tobar, Gordon Maclean, were to be made redundant.

At the same time, there was a growing sense in the local community that the arts being presented at Comar under the new regime reflected a certain disdain for island sensibilities. When a highly experimental visual art exhibition not suitable for children ran over the summer months, one local resident commented, "It was patronising, because it was like if people don't like it they just don't understand it, we're not going for a Mull audience, we're going for a global audience, so what does it matter if people on Mull don't like our art?"

Perhaps the new leadership underestimated the extent to which the Mull community had taken possession of these two much loved arts organisations. By August 2015, conflict had reached a head; a public meeting was called at Aros Town Hall in Tobermory. Over 250 angry punters arrived in minibuses from across the island to make their voices heard, so many that they could not be accommodated and a queue formed outside. A petition was presented, which had collected over 1,700 signatures in less than two days, calling for the reinstatement of the two creative directors and the resignation of the board.

In an extraordinary demonstration of popular collective action, those gathered elected an unofficial 'shadow board' made up of local residents, which would be responsible for promoting an alternative business model for Comar and placing pressure on Comar's funders and stakeholders to replace the current board with one reflecting the people of Mull. At the end of the meeting, members of the audience struck up an impromptu chorus of 'An t-Eilean Muileach', Mull's unofficial national anthem. The theatre had become much more than somewhere to go for entertainment; it was a symbol of Muileach identity, one this island community wasn't willing to let go of easily.

In the auditorium, 107 padded conference chairs are arranged on a temporary rake. A large stage allows for the mounting of productions much bigger than would typically play to a house this small. Local audiences are often the first to catch work produced by the Mull Theatre that will go on to play venues like Edinburgh's Traverse and London's Trafalgar Studios. Overhead, the plywood and timber frame of the ceiling is exposed, metal brackets uncovered, lending itself to the sense of the theatre as a working building. Tonight the auditorium is half full — or rather, half empty; this space is unforgiving when there's a small crowd. It's a sunny evening and many who might have come have likely chosen to get out their barbecues or visit the beach instead. It's the curse of the theatre professional never to be able to enjoy good weather.

The audience is curious and engaged in the show, a short clowning piece by a young physical theatre company that explores the breakdown of a marriage. Afterwards, they roll leisurely out into the evening, and their voices float up across the lawn as they descend to their cars or to walk the footpath back into town. *She was such a wonderful performer, I could watch her for hours... It sagged a bit in the middle, didn't it?*

The protest in the Town Hall was successful. The shadow board worked with Creative Scotland and Equity to put pressure on the 'official' board. By November, the trustees had all resigned, a new membership scheme was established and McCrone and Maclean had been reinstated. A new board, chaired by a local resident, was elected.

'It's tempting to see the whole story as something of an island fairytale, in which the good people of the village triumph over the dark forces of modern management-speak, and top-heavy administration,' wrote Joyce MacMillan, theatre critic of *The Scotsman*. Of course, history is written by the victors, and at times there was an unpleasant edge underpinning some of the reservations about the new leadership, a prejudice against the 'outsiders'. "Some of the things people were saying in that meeting, it was like *The Wicker Man*," says one of the team members. "I was going to avoid the *Wicker Man* comparison," I say, and she laughs. "It was just like that!" An island, after all, is also a zone of exclusion, defined not only by what it includes, but by what it keeps out.

The *Arena* crew spent several days on Mull, following the Heskeths as they went about daily life in Dervaig: doing vocal warm-ups, typing up the newsletter in a living room crowded with puppets and model boxes and piles of play texts. At one point in the documentary, the pair pad out in slippers to meet the man who has come to the house with the groceries (in spite of living in such a remote location, they never learnt to drive, and were entirely reliant on the goodwill of their fellow islanders to bring them supplies). Barrie is the more vocal of the two, passionate and a touch dramatic, while Marianne is more reflective, talking about the theatre in quiet, precise tones. They sit together, speaking to camera, physically leaning towards one another as if drawn by some magnetic force.

Then, in the theatre, they're transformed. In one scene, Barrie, clad in a hectic ginger wig and a green tartan kilt, pokes fun at the politics of the Scottish mainland, slipping between a harsh Glaswegian burr and a light Edinburgh sing-song to signal his changing characters. In another — from Aleksei Abursov's *Old World* — Marianne, elegant in a purple gown, plays a retired actress, animated in her description of past stage glories. Watching it I have some sense of the vivacity of the performances staged here; the crowd, packed into narrow rows, are uproarious, their faces glowing. It is easy to see how the theatre must have provided comfort to many in this harsh, remote environment. "One can come here alone and not feel lonely," one of the audience members comments.

But there is a note of melancholy too: a sense that the theatre has come at a cost, that they've made sacrifices in their relationship with their children, financially, and in their connection with the outside world. It has been a lonely life, Barrie explains. For all the friends they have made on Mull, the theatre has set them apart from others. "It's just been Marianne and myself, all this time," Barrie says. "Just us."

In 1979 Marianne was diagnosed with cancer. She continued to perform throughout her illness, and even undertook an extensive tour of Europe while in considerable physical pain. She died in 1984 and was buried in a plot at Calgary, an astonishing bay of white sand on the north-west coast of the island, beneath a stone bearing the words of Shakespeare's 'Sonnet 116': *Love alters not.* Barrie was heartbroken. He left the island the same year and hasn't been back since.

Many months later, I manage to track Barrie down via Facebook. Philippa, his partner, calls me and invites me to stay at their home just outside Manchester. She meets me at the station, cutting a sophisticated figure in a bright scarf and beret. On our way back to their house, she tells me something of her remarkable life story: travels across Europe; her encounter with Thomas Mann's widow, Katia; her work as a psychotherapist in 1970s Berlin; and her friendship with the author, W.G. Sebald, which she has documented in a beautiful book of her own, *Ariadne's Thread*. "Do you know, when she was a child, she played Spillikins with Heisenberg?" Barrie tells me later.

Barrie is 87, with a shock of white hair, but still bears himself with all the grace and poise of a classically trained actor. We spend the afternoon together, as he shares reminiscences of his years on Mull over tea and hot cross buns. His memory isn't as good as it used to be, he says, but he's a marvellous raconteur, recalling the details of island life with precision and humour. I can easily understand how he charmed so many people on Mull into supporting his eccentric vision.

In the evening, we sit down to a dinner of trout mousse followed by game casserole prepared by Philippa. Barrie met Philippa at Churchill College, Cambridge, where he'd taken up the offer of a residency following Marianne's death. It's obvious they have crafted a happy life together here. They trade ideas on art and history and philosophy at a dizzying rate and I struggle to keep up with the conversation in the best possible way. I spend the night in a room completely surrounded by books, occupying floor to ceiling shelves on every wall. "All the authors come out after dark. But don't worry, they're benign," Philippa says.

After losing Marianne, Barrie never acted again. "It was like she took all my interest in acting with her." His principal preoccupation in recent years has been painting. In the morning, he takes me to the basement and shows me his collection of artworks: reams and reams of them, in folders bursting at the seams, his subject matter rich and various — still life and landscapes; fantastical scenes inspired by Shakespeare and moments from his own history. I find a tiny portrait of Marianne and recognise her straight away; dressed in pink, she has a slight wave in her hair, bright eyes and an impish smile.

Barrie has been particularly interested in the question of perspective: the distinction between what we're taught to think we see — a world contained in rectangular boxes — and what we actually see. A series of works attempt to portray scenes encountered through the curvature of the cornea, lens-shaped pictures painted as if on the inside of a bowl. In several images, a dark cloud distorts the colour and image further. "That's my glaucoma," says Barrie. How characteristic of him to turn an affliction into a source of creative inspiration.

I ask him whether he misses Mull. "Mull is beautiful. But I can't go back," he says. The theatre is his legacy, but he hasn't seen its new home, although he's heard about it. I tell him how the people of Mull fought for the theatre he and Marianne created; how they stood in the town hall and sang 'An T-Eilean Muileach'.

He looks, for a moment, on the edge of tears. Then he smiles.

"Well, that's something, isn't it?" he says.

13

TARA THEATRE

London

Antique Indian doors. An earth floor. A glow-in-the-dark solar system. A bicycle. Yellow rose petals.

A TEENAGER IS TAKING A SELFIE outside Tara Theatre.

Her backdrop is a pair of doors: dark-stained wood with ornate metal work and a heavy bolt. They look out of place in this shiny new building, disrupting the eye as it skips across the grey surfaces of the street.

She looks embarrassed at my approach, giggles and scuttles off down the street. Jatinder Verma, Tara Arts' artistic director, comes out to meet me. Smartly dressed in a kurta, he is a man in possession of a magnificent beard, black flecked with silver. He sees me admiring the doors, and explains that they were imported from India, antiques that have a story to tell. "The problem with a new building is always the doors," he tells me. "They'll take years to take on the sweat and the stain of people. Old doors, well there they are: they've already got a memory, and if they are beautiful you are going to add to that memory, because people will want to touch them." They are a lure to the threshold. A way in.

Tara Theatre is situated on Garratt Lane in Earlsfield, south west London, on an awkward, end-of-terrace plot, tucked in beside the railway bridge. It couldn't feel further from the Isle of Mull, and yet, in terms of what these theatres mean to their communities, they are not so far apart. Constructed in 1891, the building was originally a draper's shop, then a Mission Hall for the railway workers. Over the years it has been a Salvation Army hall, a bingo hall and a church serving the Afro-Caribbean community. In 1983, Tara Arts took it over and turned it into a theatre.

By 2010, it was in a rather shabby state, its façade stained with pollution. Architecture firm Aedas carried out a total transformation. The theatre is still petite, but has been significantly expanded with a new extension — a tall apricot box spreading upwards from the Victorian building. The outline of a tree spreads its branches out across the frontage. Inspired by the Tree of Life, it is a motif common to mythologies around the world. Verma takes me on a tour of the building. We pass through a colourful café-bar, a rehearsal studio whose walls hang with various South Asian instruments. On the top floor is a meeting room with commanding views of the London skyline. The new theatre has won numerous awards including a New London Architecture Award and a London Construction Award, and was opened in September 2016 by London's Mayor Sadiq Khan.

Tara Arts was founded in 1977. In June of the previous year, an 18-year-old Sikh boy named Gurdip Singh Chaggar had been murdered in a racist attack in Southall. "One down, one million to go," said John Kingsley Read, former chair of the British National Front and leader of the splinter group the National Party — a comment for which a jury later acquitted him of incitement to racial hatred. The horror at the event was such that it caused a shift in attitude for many in the British Asian community — a community that had, in Verma's words, been "much more kind of law-abiding, low level — it wasn't so visible publicly". In Southall, one of the first Asian Youth Movement groups was created, and they soon began to crop up all over the country. The following summer, on 13th August, tensions came to a head at a National Front march through south east London, in what came to be known as the Battle of Lewisham. There were violent clashes between Front members and anti-racism protestors, resulting in more than 200 arrests and over 100 injuries.

Verma had recently graduated and was enraged by the racism he saw around him. He had originally arrived in Britain in 1968 from Nairobi, Kenya — the year in which Enoch Powell had made his infamous 'Rivers of Blood' speech. "I saw my mother struggling with four children in a strange land, wading through torrents of abuse, repeatedly refused rented accommodation because of the smell of her cooking, disparaged and devalued by shopkeepers and landlords, stripped of her sari and her dignity on the factory floor," he wrote in *The Guardian* in 2008.

1968 was the year my father arrived from Nairobi too, a white British boy in his early teens who had never set foot in his 'home country' before. As I chat to Verma, I wonder about the differences the two boys experienced arriving here, how my dad's white skin meant he was immediately absorbed, while Verma's heritage set him apart and caused his family to be the subject of abuse. And also, how much of it was equally disorientating and strange for them: the weirdness of seeing white bin men for the first time, the shock of the cold weather.

Verma channelled his anger into theatre. With three friends — also migrants from Kenya, India and Australia — he set up Tara Arts. Their first production was *Sacrifice*, a play about the conflict between religion and atheism by the Nobel Prize-winning Bengali poet Rabindranath Tagore. It opened at Battersea Arts Centre on 25th August 1977, less than two weeks after the Battle of Lewisham. *Sacrifice* was popular in literary circles in the 1920s, but had largely been forgotten in Britain in the intervening years. There was a significance to staging this intricate, philosophical play at a time when portrayals of Asians in British culture consisted largely of offensive stereotypes.

Tara Arts has produced dozens of shows in the years since. In 1990, Verma was the first Asian director ever at the National Theatre, where he staged Moliere's *Tartuffe*. A play about religious hypocrisy, it was especially resonant in the wake of the fatwah that had been issued on Salman Rushdie, controversial author of *The Satanic Verses*. A three-part epic exploring the migration of three generations of Indians, *Journey to the West*, toured extensively across the UK at the beginning of the millennium. And the company's staging of *The Tempest*, mined for its relevance to the experiences of colonialism, transferred to the West End in 2008. Often, the work has been seen as provocative, not only by white audiences, but also within the Asian community. Verma tells me about an occasion when Tara Arts performed at an activist meeting; there was a sketch about attitudes in the Asian community to sexuality, based on interactions they'd had while researching the show. "Halfway through, someone marched on stage and said 'this has to stop'. I told him to 'fuck off'. Strangely enough, he complied. There was deathly silence. And I ended up being beaten up. Because people felt we had traduced them. The basic argument was that, look, these are volatile times. Racism is rife. Don't clean your dirty laundry in public. Our argument was — when do you expect racism to end? And you can clean your dirty laundry in public?"

Tara Arts has been called the first British Asian theatre company, but Verma prefers to describe it as a multicultural theatre company; the emphasis, in the work, has always been on the meeting of cultures, and the power of theatre to make connections across cultures. The theatre has been somewhere not only for their own work, but where they can provide a platform for artists from a range of backgrounds — the recent programme has included work by African theatre artists and an Irish musician.

Recently, Verma contacted every person who lives on the Earlsfield Road and asked them to let him interview them about what brought them to the area. "I wasn't prescriptive at all, just stories of families and how you ended up here." He collected "a fascinating set of stories ranging from a mid-twenties person through to someone in their mid-seventies. People who've been here only a few months through to people who've been here for generations." They form the basis of *Earlsfield Stories*, a new production inspired by the lives of local people and intended to form the basis of an epic, long-term project loosely modelled on the Mahabharata.

I return later to watch the project's first incarnation. I arrive early, weighed down with a backpack full of paperwork and, somewhat incongruously, a glow-in-the-dark, 3D solar system — a gift for a friend's baby shower. I go out and sit in Tara's patio garden. A tiny triangle of space sandwiched between the building and the railway track, the garden feels like a refuge from the city — brightly coloured chairs and tables amid clusters of pot plants and tea lights tucked into recesses in the wall. A pink bicycle is propped up against an old Indian gateway.

Later, stepping into the theatre, I'm hit with a ripe scent, the pungent smell of the outdoors — somewhere wild, far from here. Over the top there's a sickly, perfumed note, the odours intermingling, coming in waves. Tara is the only theatre in the country to possess a permanent earth floor. It is a five-by-five-metre square, a rich, burnt ochre created from a mixture of Devon soil, straw and cob. Evening sunlight streams in through a lofty window, making the space glow. "I've been very taken by this particular type of red, throughout my time in the theatre, and I know now that that's from Africa, and particularly East Africa," Verma explained to me before. He was motivated, too, by the connection with the history of theatre: "it begins on the earth under the shade of a tree". The earth-floored stage seems to exist at the overlap of dimensions: indoors and outdoors, past and future, a liminal space suited to the business of drama. "Really that's what we all aspire to when we come into the theatre, we're looking for this slightly exotic out-of-body experience."

Tonight, I'm surrounded by the most genuinely diverse audience I've ever seen at a theatre — people of all ages and races. It really does look like a group of Earlsfield residents has been gathered up from the street and rounded into the stalls. Many of them seem to know each other. There's a conversation behind me about a house party going on after the performance; the host is extending invitations to others in her row. An older man, smartly dressed, with light brown skin and curls of bright white hair, keeps getting up to greet people he recognises: "nice seats, there," he says, "good view?"

The words of the Earlsfield community are performed verbatim by a cast of professional actors, an unfussy staging with the performers reading from scripts, accompanied by a pair of acoustic musicians. There are tales of weddings, children scavenging on the waste tips at Wandsworth Bridge, an eye lost during the Warsaw Uprising, a hitchhiking trip in Canada, a pianist with a broken heart.

One of the accounts belongs to Joseph, who came to Earlsfield from Guyana. He talks about how he arrived in the city in 1956, discovering, for the first time, the existence of the classes. From 1960 until his retirement in 2001, he worked for British Rail. He set up a record label too, Sun City, promoting artists from the West Indies and later, writing his own songs. He talks about meeting his wife — who had also moved from Guyana to London — how the first time he went to visit her at home, he took her beef instead of roses. "In those days it was difficult to get beef. They used to have horse meat or rabbit," he explains, and when he does so, there's a murmur of recognition in the audience. "That's right, that's how it was," someone says, and it's like that throughout the show, little ripples in the audience, the delight of seeing details you recognise from your own life acknowledged on stage.

When Joseph first arrived, he'd go to Elephant and Castle tube station and hang about for hours outside, hoping to see another person of colour. If he did, he'd approach them, and they'd swap contact details, arrange to meet up. "Racial tensions were much higher then," Verma told me, talking about that feverish summer of 1977. I'd like to believe he's right — that things are much better now. But across town, while we are sitting in this theatre, there is a disturbance in Dalston. Bins are set alight, Molotov cocktails thrown at police in riot gear. When I get home, I watch a video of it on Twitter. A lorry crashes through a barricade of upturned industrial bins and is surrounded by masked protestors who bash the windows and eventually climb on to the roof, bringing it to a halt. They are protesting the death, a few days ago, of Rashan Charles, a 20-year-old black man who died after being chased and apprehended by police. The Crown Prosecution Service will ultimately determine police officers should not face prosecution for the death. But the anger, I think, is about living in a society where it seems — in the wake of the fire at Grenfell Tower and the shooting of Mark Duggan, Jermaine Baker and Azelle Rodney — that, unconscionably, the lives of people of colour are still valued less.

In this context, the existence of this theatre feels radical and important. At the end of the show, the man in front of me — the man who was greeting the audience as they came in — gets up on stage. This, it transpires, is Joseph, and he is here to perform his song, 'World Anthem One', in public for the very first time. "I wrote three songs called World Anthem

One, Two and Three. You may ask why three World Anthems — well, the world is a big place and circumstances are not the same all over the world, each event needs its own response." He sits centre-stage, takes the microphone, and breaks into song, unaccompanied. He has a thin, sweet voice that seems to split him open and reach inside him. All around him, the audience is stilled by it, hardly breathing.

It is difficult not to think, now, of the gap between these two moments unfolding on opposite sides of the city. Preaching theatre as a solution to the world's problems might seem absurdly naïve, sentimental even — the tiny transformations I've witnessed here too little to matter. And yet I watch this man singing his anthem for the world for the very first time, his voice growing bolder as the song goes on. I look around at the faces of the audience, turned towards him, glowing orange in the light reflected from the floor. And I think: this is all there is, really. Making a clearing for a person in our midst. Allowing them to share what matters to them. Listening.

Later, in the bar after the show, the audience gathers around bowls of samosas and papadums to compare notes. I approach one of the couples featured — a young Spanish couple who met online and pursued a long-distance romance for some time before she eventually decided to move to Britain so they could be together. "How did it feel to see yourself presented on stage like that?" I ask the woman, and she giggles. She was happy, she explained, that her English sounded so good. Another woman approaches — in her 60s, neatly dressed with dark-framed glasses, fair skin and a sharp blonde bob. She tells them, "I just wanted to say thank you. I found your story very moving, very strong — especially what you said at the end." She starts crying. The Spanish woman embraces her, and the older woman sobs into her shoulder. There they are, in each other's arms, strangers holding each other, unabashed.

I only half remember what it is she said at the end, but I think it was something like: sometimes it seems that the universe is saying no. But actually, it is telling you that the things you want, you have to fight for.

At the end of the show, Verma invited the audience to walk on the stage. People shuffled out of their seats and crowded onto to the tightly packed earth. Two women discarded their sandals in the front row, put their soles directly on the ground, as if they might earth themselves. When we were all gathered, Verma said, "I promise you magic on this stage."

Suddenly, a volley of yellow rose petals rained down, and we lifted our faces skywards.

14

CONTACT

Manchester

Papadums. Pizza. A hip hop collective. The Royal College of Nursing. Graffiti. Two female footballers.

THROUGHOUT MY TEENS I was a member of Theatre Royal Bath Young People's Theatre. That was pretty much the defining thing about me. It was amazing: we staged Shakespeare and Bryony Lavery, mystery plays and beatbox theatre. We performed on the stage of the main house, we performed in the streets, we performed in National Trust properties and we performed in the toilets. I acted, wrote, made costumes, directed. When we took over *the egg*, the dedicated young people's theatre created by Haworth Tompkins, and staged a festival of our own, we had little idea of what we were doing. But we soon learned, and it was the faith of that organisation that proved to us that we could do it. We had cracking parties.

I find myself returning to the alchemy of what happened in Bath. Those years taught me how theatre actually works (have fun, learn how to collaborate, show up on time, believe in something), and what I love about it (performing, no — making, yes; Alan Ayckbourn, no — bonkers German puppet theatre, hell yes).

I'm not alone in my passion for the place where I had my first experience of being involved in theatre making. The nominations I received demonstrate how much an experience like this can shape a lifelong love with the artform, and how special the places where it happens become. Eleanor Turney nominated Theatre Peckham, explaining that here, she learned she "loved thinking about theatre and how it works".

Playwright Duncan Gates said of Malvern Theatre's youth programme, "it taught me what a personality was and how to have one."

But what happens when a theatre not only offers young people the opportunity to participate in the creation of new theatre but, moreover, places them in charge of the decision-making processes — as programmers, project leaders and even trustees? I wanted to find out, so I got on a train, and headed north.

Manchester is a city forged by change. En route from the station, I walk past new craft beer joints and hipster vintage fashion stores. Factories have been supplanted by cool blocks of flats with rows of chrome balconies. Slate grey skies full of wind-blustered blossom threaten to tip into rain.

This is the heart of the Northern Powerhouse, the Conservative enterprise designed to redress the North-South economic imbalance and to unite — as George Osborne put it — 'a collection of northern cities sufficiently close to each other that combined they can take on the world'. The BBC has recently moved into Media City in nearby Salford and tracks are being laid for the new High Speed Two rail network. Manchester is orientated towards the new; and culture, as so often is the case, is positioned at the heart of this transformation, with box-fresh arts venues like HOME and

The Factory cropping up all over the place.

I'm here to visit a theatre that has the next generation at its heart. Contact is tucked away behind a student gig venue where, tonight, The Kooks are playing. It has been described as a castle, with four huge chimney stacks almost doubling the height of the red-brick building. But it's a castle made from upturned shoeboxes and toilet rolls, with a zinc façade, rippling like a falling curtain. When I arrive, a man in a yellow van is doing a bad job of reversing into the loading bay. Two technicians look on disapprovingly.

Since 1999, Contact's unique constitution has placed young people in charge of key decision-making processes. At any one time, at least two of the board's trustees must be young people; permanent staff are always recruited through a young people's panel; and shows programmed for the theatre are selected by a panel featuring at least five young people.

Inside, the café is buzzing. I'm greeted by a group of young people, who crowd on to the table around me, jostling to tell their own stories about being part of Contact. Keisha started off here performing with a choir; within a few years she'd created her own solo show. *I Wish I Had A Moustache* explored the challenges facing young feminists and received funding from Arts Council England. Jess took part in Future Fires, a project which supports participants to create their own social engagement schemes. She established an arts club for isolated people, initially working with them one-on-one on creating their own artworks, then, as the project grew, taking them out on trips and, ultimately, mounting an exhibition.

Afreena is a first generation Mancunian Bangladeshi, the youngest daughter of the proprietor of a Moss Side curry house. She tells me her family's perception is that the theatre is somewhat seedy. "They assume that if you're performing then you're sleeping with a casting director, and it's true — just speaking truth — if you're a model, or a dancer, or anything like that — that's kind of seen as like 'it's not a good thing to do'. Because it happens in Bangladesh, well, to my parents' knowledge…Coming here was an act of rebellion," she says, although she explains her family has come to appreciate theatre more through her involvement with Contact.

The first performance she ever gave was at the Museum of Science and Industry, and was led by Repro 19, a Brazilian company who couldn't speak any English. It wasn't a barrier. "There was this one moment we were in the space and we just hugged the person next to us, and that hug, I remember, I hugged Eric, and goodness knows whatever happened to Eric but that hug was so significant, it was like no other hug I've had before or since. It was just so cool."

From then on, Afreena immersed herself in the life of the building, seizing every opportunity available to her. I know a lot about her family because she made a show about it, which toured all over the country. *Daughters of the Curry Revolution* was her first work, recalling her experiences growing up in a curry house, and her dad's tales about coming to the UK, the slipperiness of memory.

More recently, she has become a trustee of Contact, making her, effectively, artistic director Matt Fenton's boss. Like all the participants I meet, Afreena is passionate about the sense of empowerment Contact has given her. It's easy to get trapped in a bubble here, to be lulled into a false sense of security that all the world must give young women from Asian backgrounds this level of agency. But, for better and worse, it's remarkable. Afreena was reminded of this when she went to speak at an event for trustees at the National Theatre on behalf of Contact. Afterwards, she was approached by an older trustee from another major theatre. "I could just eat you up," the trustee said.

After we've spoken, I'm taken on a tour of the theatre. The layout of the building reflects the energy of the young people I meet; it's bright and disorientating. The walls are painted a frenzied pallet of violent oranges, blues and yellows, and as I wander around I never end up quite where I think I ought to be, arriving now at a mezzanine next to a digital media studio, now at a room full of teenagers eating pizza and talking about the significance of radio as a medium for political change — a topsy-turvy world populated by YouTubers, hip hop artists and social activists. At one point I attempt to return to the foyer from an upper floor, following a series of graffiti Aztec wall markings that look like arrows, before hitting a dead end. One of the teenagers asks what I'm doing and I explain. "I was just following these arrows," I say. "Oh those. They're probably left over from an immersive theatre show or something," she says.

The theatre was built in 1969 as part of the University of Manchester. Even in the early days it had a reputation for socially engaged theatre. Charlotte Keatley's 1987 feminist classic about four generations of women and their failure to connect, *My Mother Said I Never Should*, premiered here. Cathy Tyson, a graduate of Liverpool Everyman, starred in an all-black female production of *The Tempest*.

During the redevelopment of the theatre in the mid-1990s, there was a fire on the roof. The theatre was closed for much longer than anticipated and the majority of the staff had to be laid off. What could have been seen as disastrous was treated instead as a chance to reinvent, to come back better than before, like a stripped bone healing stronger in the place where it's broken. Led by chair Wyllie Longmore, who was joined in 1999 by artistic director John McGrath, the organisation began to rebuild from the foundations up, challenging themselves to find a new structure to reflect their core values.

"It's much easier to draw it on a blank sheet of paper," says Fenton, when we're talking in the café, "than to take a structure which is the inheritance of a particular kind of repertory making, and the means of production and hierarchy that was required to make that work." So Contact introduced a new way of doing things, a model of radically devolved power.

There's an extraordinary moment when you are young and you suddenly understand your own capabilities. Often it happens when someone places their faith in you for the first time. It could be as simple as getting paid for the job you've done, or being trusted with a set of keys for a building. Contact achieved it by turning the question typically asked — of how arts can be beneficial to young people — on its head. As McGrath says, "I think that the best thing to ask is what does theatre, what does culture in general, need from young people, and as soon as we start thinking about it that way you realise that it's quite a lot, there's a sense of — where's the future going? It sounds selfish but it stops it from becoming a good deed."

The creative energy that ferments at Contact spiders across the city, a network of connections and ignition points. There are the visible things. Through enterprises initiated by Contact, young people have set up a cookery course using ingredients from food banks; a five-a-side football project that teaches new migrants how to speak English; a radio station, now with three employees and 140 volunteers. All run by young people. They have nothing to do with theatre, and yet they stand on the foundations of theatre, dreamt up through the same models of creation.

They hint at all the unknowable, intangible things that are ignited here, how the business of giving a young person confidence that their voice matters and that their ideas can become manifest may have surprising impacts. Sometimes it seems to me that the least important thing that happens in theatres is the shows that get put on. Rather, it's the series of actions bringing them into being that counts.

If so many of the remarkable things that Contact is doing happen not in the theatre, but in KFC outlets and community centres across the city, does the building matter at all? For as much as a place like this provides shelter for acts of imagination to germinate, a building is also confining; a set of walls limits the action that can happen within them. I joke to Fenton that it would be awkward if they found out after they've been gone for 18 months that they don't need a building at all. He laughs, nervously. "A lot of people think that."

I ask the teenagers I'm with to tell me about the moments that stand out in their memory, moments when Contact has been at its best. As well as the shows they've loved, they talk about the accidental encounters and the things they've led to, what occurs when you're just hanging out, giving your ideas and creativity breathing space.

Sharif talks about the smoking area. After his Contact Young Company theatre sessions, he would encounter people who'd just been in hip hop and media production workshops. "Everyone would be smoking and spitting bars and rapping and dancing ... and it was a party." Some of those young people went on to form a hip hop super-collective called Levels, who have performed all over the country and are now doing a show with Manchester International Festival. There's something about the permeability of this space that fosters these kinds of spontaneous collaborations.

"For young people, I think that having a place to go is a big deal," McGrath says. "And the way in which spaces where young people can go have been excised from our society is one of the biggest challenges we face. When you look at extremism and so on, you think, how can you expect to intervene if you don't provide spaces where young people can mingle with adults outside of a hierarchical learning environment? So I do think the Contact building is really important in that way."

The show tonight, in the studio theatre, is *Offside*, a new piece by spoken word artists Sabrina Mahfouz and Hollie McNish. It tells the story of two young female footballers who play for the England team, and the prejudices they have to overcome to pursue their passions.

For many of the punters coming to Contact, it will be an experience of theatre much like any other. They pay their money, turn up and watch a show, and could walk away with no idea about the radical decision-making process behind it. But the influence of the young people is imprinted on everything that has brought them here: the ticket prices, the marketing materials, the decision, even, that this is the right show to stage.

For all this is an enterprise that benefits the young people that participate in it, my sense is that — as McGrath suggests — it is the adults who encounter the work they create who are unwittingly the beneficiaries. Fenton tells me about a performance Contact produced in collaboration with young cancer sufferers. The show explored research into the emotional consequences of living with the disease, revealing its impact on personal relationships and sexuality. The show was performed for medical colleges and, memorably, for the Royal College of Nursing national conference. At the end of the performance, the entire audience was on its feet, in floods of tears. How could it be that an experience that is so much a part of their everyday lives could generate such a response? It is because theatre acts as a searchlight, turning an unblinking gaze on the hidden parts of the human heart.

It strikes me that just about the most important thing theatre can do is to keep its faith with the young. It's no secret that the possibilities we open up to the next generation will shape not only their future, but the future we'll all inhabit. Some of those young people who pass through Contact will go on to become professional theatre-makers themselves. But many will go on to be other things: lawyers and MPs and zookeepers and train drivers. They will take the skills they have learned and use them to shape the world we live in. Have fun. Learn how to collaborate. Show up on time. Believe in something.

15

HOLBECK UNDERGROUND

BALLROOM

Leeds, West Yorkshire

The red light district. A fairy portal camp. An unseen rat. The zombie apocalypse. 120 Linda McCartney's sausages. A herd of alpacas. The shape of a pocket.

THE FIRST TIME I SAW ALAN LANE, artistic director of Slung Low, was at a conference about the relationship between theatres and their audiences. He was striding across the stage, quite literally berating the attendees — mostly senior professionals from theatres across the country for whom this was supposed to be a pleasant day out from the office, swapping anecdotes and munching pastries with their peers. In impassioned, eloquent terms he was expressing his frustration with British theatre, with its repeated failure to speak to the lives of the majority of those that pay for it through their taxes. He threw his arms about expansively, visibly angry, red in the face — a rage both intimidating and entirely magnificent.

I had just given a rather more sedate talk about why I think the continuing existence of theatres offers reasons for hope in our troubled times. I spoke about the small transformations I'd witnessed on the stage — like the time an audience member agreed to take their clothes off in an act of solidarity with the performer. I hoped that by illustrating what theatre has already achieved, I would point to what it might in the future.

But listening to Lane, I couldn't shake an unease that I was giving theatre too much free rein. After all, what is going on in a lot of theatres in this country is not the acts of generosity and bravery I was going out of my way to highlight. It is being charged too much money to watch bad musicals and thoughtless remounts of Shakespeare, an artform preoccupied not with challenging the status quo but upholding it. And if you believe theatre has the capacity not only to change people's lives but to change the world (which may or may not be the same thing), then that seems a gross dereliction of duty.

So there is reason to be angry with theatre. In *The Shape of a Pocket*, John Berger tells us, 'love is the best guarantee against idealisation'. The truth is that Lane's blistering, magnificent fury is born from the same infatuation with theatre as mine. A faith in its ability to change the world. But I wanted to see what the reality of Lane's vision for theatre is like for myself.

Slung Low's home, the HUB, is situated in Holbeck, an inner-city area of Leeds, in an industrial estate between the railway and the city. To reach it I walk through a stretch of bumpy, overgrown wasteland full of fly-tipped junk, the remnants of bonfires. It is one of those neglected spots that is, in fact, when you look closely, verdant with life; clusters of wild flowers and brambles grow here, feather-headed dandelions that bob in the breeze. The wind skims over the grass, making it shimmer like an ocean.

Beneath the railway tracks are a box factory, a car mechanics and this theatre. The HUB occupies five dusty railway arches, a stone's throw from the heart of Leeds and its shiny new office blocks, yet it seems I have entered a different realm. In the yard outside there's a stack of shipping containers, a yellow skip, an old, musty caravan, several bathtubs full of red tulips and two sheds with signs reading *The Hickling Wing* and *The Sir Peter Jonas Wing*: they contain the toilets.[1]

On the wall at the front of the site is a mural — a mosaic of broken tiles in clashing reds, greens, yellows, purples and blues. The tiles show a wild landscape of plant life and dragonflies, reflecting the wasteland opposite. The flora and fauna are sheltered beneath an umbrella, and between their leaves are insets carrying quotes: 'I'm a survivor. My whole life has been surviving'; 'I am not what happened to me. I am what I choose to become.'

These are the words of local women involved in sex work. In 2014, Holbeck made the headlines when it became the site

---

[1] Sir Peter Jonas is the former head of English National Opera who in 2015 wrote an essay entitled *ENO must live. The Arts Council should die*. It is beyond the scope of this book to unpick the complexities of the relationship between ENO and Arts Council England, but suffice it to say, Alan Lane did not share Jonas' view. Alfred Hickling is *The Guardian*'s North of England theatre critic, who, Alan says, "walked out of one of our shows after five minutes, gave his headphones back to the FOH and said, 'I thought I was coming to see theatre.' As literally the only northern-based national critic who writes for a daily he has been granted the honour of having our first toilet wing named after him. I sent him a note to come to an opening but no reply."

of the first legalised red-light district in the UK. The mural was created in 2015 by the artist Carrie Reichardt with residents alongside the volunteers and service users of Basis, a charity supporting women involved in sex work.

It is no coincidence that this is the first thing that greets you at the HUB. It's a public statement about who this place belongs to — a counterpoint to the royal arms and brass plaques bearing the names of dignitaries that adorn so many public buildings. As Lane pointed out in his talk, only the things that are valued in a place get built into the brickwork. 'TRUST ME, THIS IS ART,' states a tile in the corner of the mural.

HUB stands for Holbeck Underground Ballroom, a rather grand name that is at odds with the mildewed walls, beaten-up furniture and the occasional scurrying of a rat somewhere out of sight. But it hints at the magic that is hidden in this unlikely corner of a Leeds industrial estate. 'All are welcome — come & join the Fairy Portal Camp,' reads a sign in the foyer. As I wander through the interconnected arches, I find inexplicable curios: a full-sized, gold telephone box; an upright piano clad in a world atlas; a candyfloss machine. Near the entrance there's an old medical cabinet with *Memory Store* in red lettering above it; its recesses contain tiny jars stuffed with stories from the lives of those who have been here before me, luggage tags scribbled with snapshots of childhood daytrips, first loves and wedding days. There is also a bar where all the drinks are £1, which is about as magical as it gets.

Behind brocade curtains, the theatre takes up one of the draughty railway arches, 72 dusty tip-up cinema seats on a low rake, each seat with a plaid rug neatly folded on its back. Fairylights and rows of mismatched lampshades hang from the ceiling, and at the front a temporary black sprung floor covers the concrete. I am alone here, and for a few moments I stand on the stage and look out at the empty auditorium. The arches are reminiscent of a bunker. I imagine what this theatre could withstand. Through storms and zombie apocalypses and nuclear disasters this would be a pretty good spot to be. We'd probably have need of theatre, then; like cockroaches, theatre would be one of the last things to survive.

I think of the trains passing overhead, of all the people going about their business, completely unaware of the secret wonder beneath them. An underground ballroom hidden beneath the city. Later, looking at the map and tracing the line by which I entered Leeds with my finger, rushing up through Stalybridge, Huddersfield and Dewsbury, I realise I had been among their number.

In the event of the end of days, those that find themselves in the HUB will be well catered for. There's even a dormitory here, a basic but functional room of bunk beds with a sink, microwave and kettle, plus shelves full of books and trunks crammed with blankets. The showers are out in the Hickling Wing. For now, the beds are available to artists free of charge. The company asks few questions and rarely turns people down. Sometimes it's occupied with theatre-makers invited to perform at other venues across the city who can't afford anywhere to stay. At other times there are companies-in-residence for a week or so, living, sleeping and cooking together, spending their days developing new work in the theatre space, or plotting their zombie survival strategies.

And occasionally it's a temporary home for itinerant writers. I pass the afternoon in one of the shipping containers, writing and drinking steaming mugs of tea as rain drums on the steel roof. In the evening, I go to a gig with a friend who happens to be in town, then return late, passing through the lonely industrial estate alone and a little nervous, struggling to unlock the large metal padlock on the gate.

Inside, I unroll my sleeping bag on a bottom bunk, flick on the electric heater, switch out the light, and lie in the darkness, listening. The estate is totally silent, not even the distant sound of sirens or the ticking of old piping.

I sleep like a log. In the morning, before anyone arrives, I sit out in the courtyard in fresh, damp sunlight and breakfast on stuffed vine leaves and instant coffee amid the shipping containers and flower-filled bathtubs. I am perfectly happy.

It's Saturday afternoon and the HUB is a flurry of activity. Tonight's show is sold out, and everyone in the vicinity has been roped in to help prepare, sweeping the yard and getting dinner ready. Lane hands me a freezer bag of 120 Linda McCartney's sausages. At a picnic table, I set up two gas camping stoves and fry the sausages up in batches to add to his stew. The heat rises off them in curls of steam that condense in the cool air.

The HUB was never really intended to exist. Slung Low had grown to such a size that their funders, Arts Council England, insisted they should be working from some kind of office instead of Lane's kitchen table. The simple solution would have been to hire a floor in one of the new office blocks in town — "but for the same price, we could have all this," says Lane, with a sweeping gesture towards the five dilapidated railway arches, as he shovels up piles of rotting lino from a corner of the yard and deposits them in the skip.

Beneath the tracks of the Transpennine Express, Slung Low built a theatre, a kitchen, a workshop and the dormitory. For a time, they had a community allotment. Much more than just an office, they had created a site shared by the Holbeck community, and now the HUB plays host to a writers' group, cooking lessons and a weekly choir, as well as regular performances. This is the basic approach of Slung Low: if you are lucky enough to have something you can share, then share it. The van they purchased for a tour is insured so anyone can borrow and drive it, free of charge. A local emerging theatre company has set up a small office in an unused corner, and on the wall above their desk they've pinned a chart marking out their plans for world domination.

Everyone who works with Slung Low earns exactly the same, including Lane — £500 per week, the average wage in this part of the country, he points out. Performances are all pay-what-you-decide, which might very well mean some audience members pay nothing, although many pay far more than they might usually have been charged. A free hot meal is a regular feature of a night out at the HUB.

The simple act of inviting a person to be in a shared space, of feeding and entertaining them in an exchange that is not principally economic — of valuing their presence in measures other than commercial — is striking because it is so rare. It is a reminder that, to paraphrase theatre academic Jen Harvie, even though capitalist conditions are widespread, they are not totalising and can be disrupted.

Perhaps it took a company dedicated to making work outside of conventional performance spaces to create this. Slung Low's own shows have been staged in car parks, warehouses and town squares — but rarely in theatres. Right now, they are in the middle of making a year-long epic called *Flood*. Part of the celebrations marking Hull Capital of Culture 2017, *Flood* tells the story of two local fishermen who haul from the depths of the ocean a mysterious woman called Gloriana. It is a play about migration, about what it means to find your way far from home, set against the backdrop of a great storm that is sweeping the world. The live show features a cast of 99, four boats, a 10-metre petrol explosion, marine flares, and will be performed on a floating set in 30,000 cubic metres of water in Hull's Victoria Dock.

Slung Low was formed in 2000 and grew into a collective of 36 young artists, an umbrella for a bunch of people who wanted to make theatre together. Even then, they were vaultingly ambitious, wishing to stage work on an epic scale which ruled out the conventional small theatres where companies usually start out. "You can't enter on a Landrover in a studio," says Lane. So they put their plays on elsewhere. Because the performances happened not in settings designated for the purpose of theatre, but where ordinary people go about their everyday lives, their work was suddenly being seen and enjoyed by people who would never see themselves as theatre-goers. It became as much about who gets to experience their shows as the kind of theatre they were making, an intertwined politics and pragmatism characteristic of Slung Low's ethos.

It makes sense that this impromptu theatre operates on such a matter-of-fact basis — rough and ready, open to pretty much anyone who wants to use it. It exists, for now, because people seem to find it both useful and delightful. Lane is clear that it will continue to do so only for as long as this is the case; there will come, he tells me, a time when both the company and the venue have served their purpose, at which point, they will close.

This gets to the heart of what Slung Low is: an entity that can expand to the largest dream of the people that inhabit it, but never any bigger. It reveals to me a wider problem with institutions, from banks and newspapers to entire economic systems: they go wrong when they outsize people and can no longer be controlled by them, like so many runaway juggernauts. Theatres can be a salve to a world of institutions-gone-rogue, as long as they stay people-sized, the shape of a pocket.

Berger again: 'The pocket in question is a small pocket of resistance. A pocket is formed when two or more people come together in agreement. The resistance is against the inhumanity of the new world economic order ... unexpectedly, our exchanges strengthen each of us in our conviction that what is happening to the world today is wrong, and that what is often said about it is a lie.'

It's satisfying to think, as I stand cooking sausages in the open air, that I might be making a better world possible.

At 6.30 p.m. the HUB starts to fill up. Guests are getting

their names ticked off the list and buying cheap bottles of lager from the bar. It's cold in here, so Lane stokes up the woodburning stove, chucking in chunks of old set that are no longer required. We sit too close, and my face glows with the heat while the rest of my body stays icy.

The guests settle in, pulling rugs over their laps, laughing and chatting, so the atmosphere in the auditorium is more like a sleepover than a night at the theatre. Tonight's show is *The Best of BE Festival*: three short performances representing the best of European contemporary theatre, with young companies from France, Germany and Italy, unknown here but met by a curious, receptive crowd.

In the interval, we sit together at the long, gingham-covered tables and tuck into bowls of bean, sausage and maple syrup stew, served up by the Slung Low team from a vast pot. I get chatting to the guy sitting opposite me. "I just always come here, whatever's on — it's my place," he says, and then we start trading ghost stories, because there's nothing that theatre people love more than ghost stories.

Eating together is a great leveller, I think, as we pass around chunks of crusty white baguette. It is the quintessential human experience, the one thing you can be certain we hold in common. Once you've eaten alongside someone, they are no longer a stranger. A meal is a deceptively simple kind of gift, and I suspect that's why Lane is so exacting in his insistence on all these small acts of munificence — because they express something bigger than the sum of their parts. It's the sign you nail to the front gate.

After the performance there's a question and answer session with the performers. The guests are inquisitive and thoughtful, the questions and answers become a real conversation, and it's hard not to feel that the enthusiasm on both sides is tempered with an air of melancholy, knowing that, among all the other, complicated things that Britain's exit from the EU may, in future, make gatherings like this harder to organise — and so more important than ever. Lane and the rest of the Slung Low team are not here. They're out in the kitchen, doing the washing up.

Late at night, after the show, Lane and I are in his car, driving through the Yorkshire countryside. "The dorm will be good for the book, sure, but come and stay with us afterwards, you'll be more comfortable," he had said, when he learnt about my trip — a characteristic act of care towards a person he'd met precisely once before, at a conference in Manchester. And he was right; staying in the back bedroom of the old terraced policeman's cottage he shares with his wife and his toddler son who likes to dance to Ed Sheeran, full of books and music and the chickens he rescued from a factory farm, is *wonderful*.

Yesterday, Lane took me to the highest point of the

Holme Valley. We gazed out across it, one of those vast, humbling landscapes that reminds you how small we really are. We took his dog for a long walk across fields and through woodland, turning back on ourselves when we encountered a herd of mean-looking alpacas. "You may have won the battle, but I'll win the war," Lane told them.

As we walked, we talked about what it means to stand up for what you believe in and in a way it frightened me because I could see how it demands an integrity I'm not sure I'm capable of; to live, so unwaveringly, like this. I could see how my willingness to compromise, rather than being a strength, might actually be the crack where the leak begins.

Now, the Yorkshire countryside streaks past the window, shrouded in darkness. A weird peel of apricot moon balances on the horizon. Somehow we get talking about his dad, who died, suddenly, when Lane was in his early 20s. Around the same time, Lane himself was diagnosed with Hodgkin's Lymphoma, a cancer that attacks the lymphatic system.

At 22 he underwent a stem cell transplant. For three months he was alone in a room, without human contact save two medical staff, wondering if he would survive, knowing, in fact, that it was more likely he would not. The only way he got through it, he says, was to imagine a time when the agonisingly slow seconds and minutes would become the story he would tell in the future, the story he would tell to make sense of how he got through them. The story he is telling me now.

It seems crude to attribute Lane's sense of what is important to these experiences. I don't doubt he was righteous and blazing when he was a teenager too. But he says that what was demanded of him to get through the long days alone in that room, more than anything else, was good spirit, and perhaps something of that good spirit was not only knowing that he had to live, but what he had to live for.

"Principles only have value when they become difficult to stick to. When people would forgive you for choosing to compromise, but you don't," he says. Principles are, in and of themselves, the inverse of what the capitalist system we operate within demands of us, because they hold that people are capable of being motivated by commitments greater than their own gratification.

Berger said that love is the best guarantee against idealisation. What that means, in practice, is resistance; resistance to compromise, resistance that is costly and painful. It means that the things we love are not only worth fighting for, but perhaps that the fight for that which we love is the only thing that has worth.

In the darkness, I ask Lane what he sees as his guiding principle.

"Don't be craven," he replies.

It is the shape of a pocket.

16

THE CENTURY THEATRE

Coalville, Leicestershire

A gallows frame. 10,000 paper clips. Chelsea blue paint. The Daily Worker. A bombsite.

I HAD NEVER HEARD OF the Century Theatre until a friend mentioned it to me in passing one day over lunch. A theatre on wheels that travelled the length and breadth of the country in the wake of the Second World War, taking performances to communities that had no theatre of their own. The notion spoke to my sense of theatre as something basic and necessary — a kind of touchstone that, in the wake of cataclysmic events such as war, we return to. But I couldn't quite imagine the logistics of how a thing like that could be made to work. She wasn't, after all, describing a miniature puppet theatre or a soft-sided *spiegeltent*, but a full-scale auditorium and stage, complete with dressing rooms and wings, as lavishly equipped as any decent theatre of the day. And so it acquired in my mind the patina of a myth, something belonging to a different world where the normal bounds of physics didn't quite apply — or at least not the regulations of the Highways Authority.

Researching online, I discovered that the Century Theatre, many years after being declared unfit to travel Britain's roads, still exists, immobilised on a former industrial site in North West Leicestershire. It even has a programme of public performances. I had to check it out for myself to learn what the visits of this theatre had meant to communities still healing; and to get my head around how it actually worked.

John Beasley meets me at the bus stop beneath the clock tower in Coalville, an old mining town that is now largely sustained by a collection of warehouses, including Amazon's biggest fulfillment centre in the UK. Beasley is one of the volunteers that keeps the old theatre operating. Clad in a black shirt and a faded baseball cap emblazoned with the slogan *Old Guys Rule*, he throws open the door to his Peugeot, pushing aside a clutter of flyers and CD cases to make room for me.

The Century Theatre is now permanently housed at the site of the old Snibston Colliery, a short distance from town. We pull up at an automatic gate and it clanks open slowly. The site seems rather desolate in the baking sun, a dust-blown expanse of concrete — the footprint of the former Snibston Discovery Museum, a venue dedicated to 500 years of technological innovation, which was dismantled a year ago. A security guard dozes in a solitary shack.

A single disused railway line runs through the site. One of the oldest lines in the country, built by the great railway engineer Robert Stephenson and opened in 1836, it was used to transport the coal extracted from the Snibston Colliery to Leicester. Here is the old gallows frame, its wheels long since stilled but the cable even now taut on the hoist. The remains of the original colliery, and this adjoining railway, are a listed heritage site — which is handy for the proprietors of the theatre, because it means the location is protected from the advances of commercial property developers. There's an aura of obsolescence, a gathering of articles past their sell-by-date. Indeed, the Century Theatre ran aground here in 1996. Following changes to traffic regulations in 1974, it was no longer deemed roadworthy and, having spent more than two decades stationed by Derwent Water in Keswick, Cumbria, was in need of a seemly spot for its retirement. Nearby, a yard full of unfathomable machine parts molders quietly, slowly being overwhelmed by clouds of buddleia.

Tucked away behind rows of neat, new-build semis, the yard feels removed from the traffic of the town: not the kind of setting in which you would expect to find a theatre. And yet, here it is — and thriving.

The Century Theatre is a bright blue structure, a shade darker than the brilliant summer sky. It is much bigger than I had imagined, comprising four ex-military trailers that have been carefully aligned in parallel, their sides folded down to form one continuous platform internally, containing the seating and stage. To maintain the precise, 10-degree rake of the seating, the rear trailers have been hoisted up on a crude platform of jacks, scaffolding poles and stacked railway sleepers, "the same railway sleepers they were using in the 1950s," Beasley tells me, proudly.

It's a Heath Robinson invention; a structure formed around the pragmatic needs of the performance space rather than with a particular consideration for beauty. It looks heavy, botched together — it's almost impossible to think of it trundling through the streets of Britain, a caravan of 19 trailers travelling at 15 miles an hour. And yet, that's what it was — a theatre on wheels, designed to bring the artform to the widest possible audience. The vision of the Century Theatre was to expose communities that had lost theatres or never had them to drama 'of indisputable merit'. In the wake of the Second World War, there was a revival of travelling theatre companies, who would perform in village halls, schools and churches — wherever crowds of people might congregate. But the Century promised a different kind of experience, with all the comfort and trappings that a more traditional night out at the theatre might offer, presenting fully realised productions with substantial sets and lighting designs.

In his insightful book, *The Blue Box, The Story of the Century Theatre 1947-1983*, Alan Hankinson tells the story of how John Ridley brought this unlikely vision into being. An engineer in a Hinckley factory, before the outbreak of War Ridley had worked in the theatre as a stage manager, director and producer. Once he had taken on his 'proper' job, he couldn't quite shake theatre loose, that insidious way it has of creeping under the skin like a microbody, and he dedicated much of his free time to sketching out the model for a mobile theatre.

For every problem posed by his brainchild he would

dream up an inventive solution. On drafting paper he outlined the plans for his theatre, a huge caterpillar unfolding in a series of angled planes and elevated on jacks and wheels. Even on the page it looks unwieldy; the narrow trailers seem liable to topple beneath the weight they carry. Was this something he genuinely believed might one day be built, or nothing more than a mental exercise, a way of whiling away unfilled time before the advent of Netflix and Sudoku?

The war ended and in its wake the country was gripped by a new sense of confidence and opportunity. Ridley's madcap scheme began to look credible when, in 1947, he met Wilfred Harrison and Richard Ward, two actors with the Adelphi Players who were in town to perform at the Hinckley Working Men's Club. The men complained of the nuisances of life on the road — having to lug all your own gear about, turning up in strange venues with no sense of what performing conditions might be like. Ridley showed them his plans, and the two men were persuaded to come on board, joining the project as financial secretary and director of productions respectively.

'Mechanically impossible, artistically impossible, financially impossible,' Ridley claimed Arts Council of Great Britain had said of the enterprise. Yet I imagine these words would, if anything, have solidified his resolve. He was a man of quiet determination, persisting against mounting odds. In 1948 he quit his job at the factory to dedicate himself to the project, sinking a sizeable chunk of his own capital into the purchase of several ex-military vehicles. Through a savage winter, the trailers were transformed into something that suggested a theatre.

A photograph on display at the theatre shows him at work with Rob Robinson, whom he had engaged to assist him. They are gazing down intently at a stretch of cable they're working on; Ridley's lips pursed in concentration, extravagant eyebrows furrowed. He looks like a youthful John Hurt with a neat, Lenin beard, his pale face framed with a beret, set at a jaunty angle. Beneath his intense concentration, I can trace the faint ephemeron of a smile — he was aware, perhaps, that he was being photographed, a performance of industry, everyone in on the joke.

Without support from the newly formed Arts Council of Great Britain, the project was funded piecemeal, with small contributions from around a thousand donors. They received, too, donations of crucial material items: electric cable, steel sheets and piping; a gas cooker; a sewing machine; 10,000 paper clips; and the bright Chelsea blue paint that earned the theatre its enduring nickname, The Blue Box. I suspect it was the very unfeasibility of the project — so worrisome for the Arts Council of Great Britain — that appealed to its multiple patrons. 'I think even the most sanguine of us came away with a few mental reservations, but there was something about those young men that warned us not to be too knowing,' wrote *Punch*'s Eric Keown, who saw the plans for the theatre at the 1949 British Theatre Exhibition.

By 1952, the theatre was ready to take to the road. Its strength had been tested by 225 teenagers from a local school, who had been roped in to jump up and down in the auditorium. It must have been some sight, trundling through the towns and villages of the UK, Crossley tractors pulling up to three trailers with a total length of over 30 metres, a caravan of wagons and living vans behind them. Often a group of the Centurions would have to get out to lever one of the trailers around a tricky corner, and Ridley invented a metal frame that stood erect from the top of the first tractor, to ensure the convoy would clear any low bridges they encountered en route.

The doggedly unbeautiful exterior makes what you find when you step into the auditorium all the more astonishing. A perfectly formed, 206-seat theatre (originally 225), rows of moss-coloured velvet seating, raking gently down to the stage. The aisles are carpeted in red pile, and the walls painted heritage green. The only indication that this isn't a theatre with its feet firmly planted on the ground is a set of four thick, black iron bars that jut up through the aisles and hold the entire structure together.

Recently the theatre has been upgraded. A brand new foyer and bar area has been added, a two-storey prefab building with an air-conditioning system that is most welcome on this baking day. Beasley invites me to step on to the stage while he demonstrates the new LED lighting, of which he's clearly very proud. Then, he cranks open the red velvet curtains, plays a loud blast of the can-can over the high spec sound system and encourages me to join in, "to get a sense of what it would have been like to perform here." I oblige — perhaps not as enthusiastically as I might — and over the speakers comes a chorus of uproarious applause and shouts of encore, which echo strangely around the empty auditorium.

The Century finally opened at Hinckley in 1952 with a production of *Othello*. It received a flurry of attention from the national media, who were fulsome in their praise for the unlikely enterprise. Later, the repertoire grew to include works such as *Twelfth Night* and Moliere's *The Miser*. Each season featured three different shows on rotation. In the first year they visited Warwickshire, Oxfordshire, Gloucestershire, Worcestershire, Shropshire, Staffordshire and Cheshire.

How fine to set out on the highway, your entire life packed up in a mobile bedsit. I imagine the company members must have felt unfettered; after the strictures of life during the War it's easy to understand the appeal of life on the road. The same spirit as running away with the circus — a flipped birdie at a life that, for young people particularly, had been restrictive, even fatal. They were a transient community, bound by their passion for their art, a hunger for new destinations and the unfurling ribbon of cement beneath their wheels.

From their elevated perch in the cabs of the trailers, they witnessed a country still recovering from war. They would have passed abandoned military bases, bombsites, unrepaired buildings — open wounds still exposed to the elements. They arrived in locations that were scarred and roughly patched up, communities still living with rationing and austerity. But there were signs of renewal too. New high-rise buildings and blocks of prefab council housing were being erected; whole new towns like Stevenage and Harlow were being mapped out. The 1951 Festival of Britain had captured the pervasive spirit of optimism, a forward-facing outlook that proposed a better future built on egalitarian principles, breaking down the social divisions of the past.

The communities they arrived in were hungry for the return of the theatre they had lost in the war (many venues had either been bombed out or closed due to fears about bombing), even in spite of the competing attractions of cinema and the arrival of television in affluent homes. The Century Theatre was greeted by enthusiastic audiences. The erection of the strange structure became an attraction in itself, generating momentum for the show to be performed. As the Century's reputation grew, so did audience numbers. In Burnley, it drew a particularly impassioned crowd of teenaged fans, who wrote to the local paper demanding the publication of photographs of that season's artistic director, Braham Murray (subsequently a founder of Manchester Royal Exchange). A few months later, when the council decided not to offer the necessary financial guarantee to secure the Century's return, 50 young people marched on the town hall, brandishing banners with slogans such as 'Ban the Bomb — not the Century'. The Mayor emerged to meet them and gave his reassurances that the theatre would be back.

What role did theatre play in the lives of a people still wounded, but ready to imagine a better future? In the post-war years, more than ever there was room for drama that spoke to the lives of ordinary people. The Arts Council of Great Britain had been founded in 1946 with the aim of increasing access to the arts. Enterprises like the Unity Theatre movement brought theatre to more people than ever before. In 1956, John Osborne's seminal play *Look Back in Anger* placed the lives of young, disaffected, working-class men centre-stage. Theatre was becoming a setting where people of all backgrounds could see their own lives reflected back at them.

Although the plays presented by the Century Theatre were not particularly leftfield, what I think was significant was the readiness of the company to take drama to communities frequently excluded from the arts. They performed, Harrison told Hankinson, in 'a field in Chipping Norton, cattle market in Rugby, public park in Warwick, municipal gardens in Cheltenham, a school yard, bomb site, slum clearance area'. The egalitarian spirit of the time extended to the way the company operated. Everyone working for the Century earned the same — initially around £2 a week — and they lived in identical bedsits, two to a caravan, with a shared shower and toilet. When they weren't on stage, they'd be doing publicity, the cooking or the washing up — whatever the organ of the theatre required. It was a genuine cooperative, in tune with the optimistic socialist spirit of the nation. As the Communist newspaper *The Daily Worker* reported, 'no company in Britain can have a more truly communal life'.

One of the biggest jobs was dismantling the theatre and packing it up ready for the journey to its next destination. Like everything about keeping this monolithic cavalcade moving, it was an arduous process lasting at least eight hours. As they laboured in thick mud, into the night, the Centurions must have asked themselves whether they wouldn't be better off landing a well-paid gig in a theatre with real foundations or a part in one of the shows on the newly flourishing television stations.

Getting by on such a meagre salary was tough, too. In time, the egalitarian ethos of the outfit began to disintegrate;

the company divided into actors and stage managers, with many of the former less willing to participate in the process of dismantling and moving the theatre as they had in the past. 'One long crisis on wheels,' John Mapplebeck dubbed the theatre in *The Guardian* in 1960. Still, they forged on, just about managing to sustain the forward propulsion of the organisation by drawing on the goodwill of their supporters — and a hefty overdraft. In 1974, when legislation governing road traffic changed, it ran aground in Keswick, where it was to stay for 22 years before its final move to Coalville.

It is poignant to see the Century Theatre like this, immobilised in a ruined industrial estate like a stranded boat at low tide. But in fact it is enjoying a thriving, busy life. Thanks to the dedication of a team of highly committed volunteers like Beasley, the Century Theatre opened its doors as a working venue again in 1997, and has been run by volunteers ever since, with a regular bill of cinema screenings, stand-up comedians and touring theatre shows.

I return a few months later to see the theatre in action. Beasley is standing in the foyer in a branded Century T shirt. He greets me warmly, before returning to front-of-house duties. It's busy this evening with a crowd dressed for a big night out. As we make our way into the auditorium, I overhear conversations about football and dieting. "I was disappointed last week. I'd gained a pound."

We're here for a stage adaptation of *Steptoe and Son*. Accompanied by a blast of The Rolling Stones' 'Paint it black', the red curtain sweeps open, with the grace of a breath (the motorised track system is a new addition since I was last here). I've never seen the TV show, so it's weird encountering it for the first time in imitation. The humour is dated — much of it with an uncomfortable homophobic undertone. *Steptoe and Son* was the entertainment of choice in the early 1960s, when the Century Theatre was in its prime. It seems, suddenly, like a very long time ago. But the theatre itself is no period piece — it still works perfectly, and there is little clue to the fact we are actually sitting inside a row of ex-military trucks. The seats are more comfortable than in many West End theatres.

In the bar after the show, Beasley introduces me to the other volunteers on duty tonight. They ask me how they might make a more experimental, contemporary programme work here. They'd like to do it, but worry it would be off-putting for their audiences. It's flattering to be asked. I have no idea. They start riffing on the idea of a musical about Action Man, the toy figure first created by a Coalville based company in 1966. Their passion for this enterprise is clear. None of them comes from an arts background. One volunteer has worked for the council for years, another spent his life "firing high voltage electricity at things". I ask them what motivates them to keep at this, giving up hours of free time every week to keep it running. "It's like a drug," one of the group tells me. "If you went back to the beginning and met the people who started this, the spirit now — it's almost identical."

The next morning, I drive over to the Wigston Record Office, where the Century Theatre's archive is kept. On the website, there is the tantalising promise of a wooden demonstration model of the theatre, designed to illustrate how it fitted together, but it's nowhere to be found. "I think you're the first person that's ever asked for it," the archivist says. What I discover instead are press cuttings, boxes and boxes of them, mostly uncatalogued, overwhelming evidence of how this unlikely theatre captured the public imagination. Not just local newspapers but all the nationals, as well as *World Science Review*, *English Electric* and *Move* — the magazine of the commercial vehicle and road transport club. Articles from French newspapers and the USSR's *Teatr* magazine. One young reporter for a Rochdale newspaper, 21-year-old Patricia Banes, was so taken with it all — and with actor Terence Carter — that she quit her job and ran away with the Century Theatre, becoming the manager's secretary. In the words of *The Farmers' Weekly*, 'The world would be a dull place if it weren't for people like John Ridley who throw sense and security to the wind and follow an ideal.'

Not everyone was persuaded by the Century Theatre's

story. A returned manuscript submitted by Harrison to the BBC in 1977 is scrawled with the words, 'This is fucking nonsense. I'm not satisfied it's genuine.' Harrison sent an admirably circumspect reply: 'When the Century Theatre was first mooted, over 25 years ago, 'they' didn't believe it possible. And now, it seems, 'they' don't believe it ever happened. Thus history is re-written by the unimaginative.'

17

THEATRE BY THE LAKE

Keswick, Cumbria

A herd of black sheep. A headless tailor's dummy.
Midnight skinny dippers. William Wordsworth.
A single star.

Keswick, 24ᵗʰ April 2017

Yesterday I walked along the eastern shore of Derwentwater, past the pontoons to a beach littered with sharp rocks. I dipped my toe, and, deciding to brave it, stripped down to my swimsuit and clambered in, my footsteps precarious on weed-covered rocks. I paused as it rose over my hips, before taking the plunge, my skin singing with the bald shock of the water. This confrontation with the liquid world always seems to 'bring me to my senses', in the most literal way; I feel mind and body and the natural environment are restored in a moment to their correct alignment.

I kicked out into the lake, the cool seeping into my skin, mellowing the heat of my blood. As I swam, I took in the mountains, vast and distant, dashed by cloud shadows, and I could just make out the roof of the theatre, protruding over treetops. Then, shifting my focus, I saw the minute floatsam of the water's face, dancing dust particles, an errant swan's feather, skittering back and forth across the surface. Roger Deakin wrote in Waterlog *of having a 'frog's eye view'. It's the only way to be in a place like this: not only in nature, but beneath its surface, enveloped by it.*

People looked down at me from the path and hollered 'someone's swimming there, you're crazy!' and I shouted up, telling them 'it's cold but it's fine when you go a bit numb'. Then my skin started to grow hot which I was immediately certain was a warning sign of hypothermia, so I panicked, swam back to the shore and clambered out, watched by onlookers in puffa jackets, some arsehole with a drone. The air now seemed, to me, magnificently warm. Luxuriating in it, I sat down on a rock, then opened a flask of coffee as I waited for the sun to dry me off.

Now, it's snowing. In retrospect, it was probably a bit cold to go swimming yesterday.'

§

KESWICK IS A MARKET TOWN with a population of just 5,000, situated in Cumbria, one of the most sparsely populated counties in Britain. Nearly 20 miles from the rail link at Penrith, to reach it I take a bus that trundles through expanses of green fields and tumbledown stone walls. A herd of black sheep with white heads glances up as we pass.

When the Century Theatre was finally declared un-roadworthy in 1975, it ran aground here, in a lakeside car park, and ended up staying until 1996, when it was moved to Coalville. A few years later, in 1999, Theatre by the Lake opened, metres from where the Century had stood. It's an unlikely setting for a performance venue. In the words of founding executive director Patric Gilchrist, "it's a very eccentric proposition, really, because no strategic plan would come up with the idea of sticking a theatre there."

But the Lake District has always had a close relationship

with the arts. I stroll down to where the theatre stands on the edge of Derwentwater. Looking out across the lake, I see a claude glass landscape, framed by romantic evocations that have slipped into cliché, as if Wordsworth, Coleridge and all the others had not only documented this place, but somehow conjured it into being. In the shallows, amateur photographers with their trousers pushed up to their knees are crouching, attempting to find new angles on the view.

The theatre is hidden behind a bank of plane trees, a handsome, three-storey structure that sinks into the Cumbrian countryside. The brickwork is the grey stone common to this part of the country, with sections roughcast and limewashed, a blue-black slate roof, and a squat fly tower, the tallest planning regulations would allow. The entrance is a tall, glazed box that allows those standing inside on the first and second floors to gaze back out into the landscape, across the fields opposite that slope gently to the water. Recently, a pavilion has been added to house the café, a timber and glass construction with a stone hearth at its centre. The architecture is designed to blend into the background, as the Park Authority required. "Apparently, the chief planning officer at the time drew a sketch on the back of an envelope, and it was a sort of Lakeland barn," Gilchrist says. It gives the impression that you could stroll straight from the fells into the stalls without stopping to take your boots off.

The Century Theatre had provided impetus, but in fact

the campaign for a permanent venue here had been running, intermittently, since 1964. Over the years, various proposals had been made — one for a theatre in Keswick's old railway station, another for Derwent Island in the middle of the lake. It was only with the advent of the National Lottery in the early 1990s, and new funding streams for capital projects of this nature, that it became viable. Not all were in favour of the scheme. "There were letters in the *Keswick Reminder* about 'this excrescence, down by the lake'," Gilchrist tells me. "They were objecting to change, essentially, and the scale of the building was unlike anything Keswick had experienced since the coming of the railways." Eventually, after years of hard wrangling with the Park Authority, permission was granted. Construction started in 1998, supported by a National Lottery grant of £4.5 million and £1.5 million from other sources. Supporter Judi Dench was photographed on site, smiling from behind the wheel of a JCB digger.

Gilchrist joined the project in the summer of 1998, when it was little more than "a hole in the ground". A year later, on 16th August 1999, he was handed the keys. "Most of the things worked some of the time," he says. Two days later, a special dress rehearsal was staged for the builders who worked on it. "They only saw the first half of the show. They spent the second half in the bar, but they had great pride in it," Gilchrist says. "You still get guys who worked on it coming in and checking it out. Because it was probably the most significant building any of them had worked on." The next day, the theatre opened its doors to the public. It was an immediate success. By the second year 120,000 people were visiting annually, defying projected figures of around 60,000. Gilchrist estimates that around 60% of the theatre's audiences are Cumbrian locals. "One of the things that was said to me while we were building it was 'you can't programme it through the winter. Nobody in Cumbria goes out during the winter' — well, it can only have been because there was nothing to do." More than 18 months passed before the theatre 'went dark' for a brief period, with no performances taking place so essential maintenance work could be carried out.

Artistic director Conrad Lynch meets me in the lobby before taking me on a swift tour of the theatre. Backstage is a warren of offices, dressing rooms and loading bays, that mystifying profusion of rooms that are, Narnia-like, accommodated out-of-sight in the hidden parts of theatres. The tiny, claustrophobic wardrobe department is stuffed with shelves of overspilling boxes labelled in black Sharpie: braid, fringe and tassels, broderie anglaise, bias binding, men's pants, bras, lace collars and bits. A naked, headless tailor's dummy stands in the corner.

Stepping on stage in the main house, we pause and gaze

out at the auditorium— 389 seats, each with a great view of the stage, surrounded by wood panelling and an orchestra pit. The seats are upholstered in varying shades of tomato, terracotta and salmon, much easier on the eye than a single wall of red — and kinder to an actor performing to a house that isn't full.

Theatre by the Lake's programming ethos is reflected in its tagline, 'The Drama of the Lakes'. Successful shows developed and staged here include Melvyn Bragg's *The Hired Man*, a musical depicting working-class Cumbrian life at the turn of the 20th century. An adaptation of James Rebank's *The Shepherd's Life* in 2015 captured a harsh, visceral means of existence that has been intrinsic to the Lake District for over 5,000 years, far removed from its tea rooms and pleasure cruises. A herd of puppet sheep, created by one of the team behind *War Horse*, populated the stage; stepping outside in the interval for a breath of fresh air, the audience came face-to-face with the real thing — Herdwicks grazing in Crow Park, by the water's edge.

Alongside the main house, Theatre by the Lake boasts a studio theatre where smaller and riskier shows are mounted. The stage is set for tonight's performance of *Two Way Mirror*, a duo of short, lesser-known Arthur Miller plays. The double bill has recently returned to the venue following a tour of village halls and rural community centres. Theatre by the Lake keeps the heritage of the Century alive in this way, sending companies out on the road to visit the tiny communities scattered across Cumbria. Every venue on the tour has sold out and they're the most fun gigs for the company to play. "Show reports come in saying 'the second half went up late because of the 'dark passions buffet'' or 'stage management won the wine in the raffle this evening'," Lynch explains.

It's less than an hour until the show is due to start and backstage is a flurry of activity, actors hurrying about, performing rushed vocal warm-ups and adjusting costumes. Working in such a remote location presents some practical problems for a producing house, not least of all the provision of actors. Ian Forrester, the founding artistic director of Theatre by the Lake, made the decision early on to mount plays using the repertory model. Each summer, between 10 and 15 actors spend seven months here, staging six new plays, so by the end of the season audiences can see a different show every night of the week. This approach, in which a resident company of actors presents a 'repertoire' of plays across a season, has since crept back into fashion at venues like the Liverpool Everyman. Practical considerations led the decision at Theatre by the Lake — there isn't a resident population of professional actors nearby, so it was a necessary means of producing their own plays.

What they discovered is that the intimacy that develops

between the actors lends the work on stage a different kind of fluency. The proximity to the lakes is significant too; it seeps into the company members and manifests on stage. "Somehow that aura, and pride of place, that comes through," Gilchrist says. What an adventure it must be to arrive for a season, in *Swallows and Amazons* territory, for a summer among the lakes and mountains. You have to put your life on hold if you sign up for this; after the first six weeks, once the plays are up and running, there's no escape. Performing until late on Saturday night, and then back in rehearsals first thing on Monday morning, you have no chance to get away. So you spend your downtime sailing and climbing, falling in love with your fellow cast members, then out of love again, partying at The Loft — Keswick's premiere (and only) nightclub. Skinny dipping in the lake at midnight.

Isn't this what so appeals about this landscape: the promise of evading the real world? How easily the frustrations of everyday life might be left behind? One of the cast arrives through a back door, naked to the waist, wrapped in a small towel, skin covered in goosebumps, and shakes a veil of water droplets from a mane of dark curly hair. He's just been swimming. I ask him how it was. "Wonderful!" he says. Tomorrow, I'll follow in his strokes, writing in my diary afterwards, '*my skin started to grow hot which I was immediately certain was a warning sign of hypothermia. In retrospect, it was probably a bit cold to go swimming...'*

At 7.30 p.m., the auditorium is filling up. Earlier, Lynch and I spoke about how it's one of the most thrilling moments for a theatre professional, waiting in an empty auditorium for an audience to arrive. Watching them all file in, taking their seats, flicking through the programme, chatting to their neighbours. I think about an episode in a book I've recently been reading, Ben Lerner's *The Hatred of Poetry*. In it, he describes attending theatre, this instant on the cusp of the play's beginning, how as the lights dimmed he 'felt that other worlds were possible, felt all my senses sharpened, that some of them were melding with those of the other kids ... in the dark beside me'. He is drawing a parallel with the 'hatred' referred to in his book's title: the gap between the metaphysical potential of 'poetry' as an abstract notion, and the disappointment caused by the inevitable failure of any individual poem to reach it — because it strives for a sound and expression that are beyond human ken. He quotes John Keats: 'Heard melodies are sweet, but those unheard/Are sweeter; therefore, ye soft pipes, play on/Not to the sensual ear, but, more endear'd/Pipe to the spirit ditties of no tone'.

And yet, here — in this gap where the attempt is made — lies the beauty. This is what the auditorium represents in these breaths before the show begins: potential. Lerner calls this 'the little clearing the theater makes'. It's a fine way to describe the artform.

Lerner doesn't mention William Wordsworth, but his work was reaching for a lost potential too. 'Our birth is but a sleep and a forgetting,' he writes in *Ode: Intimations of Immortality*, a poem about our lost connection with the transcendental beauty of nature. Through his poetry, he endeavoured to take possession of nature, as if with language he could fix it, pin it down.

The play tonight focuses on the personal struggles Wordsworth faced through the events of 1812, when two of his children died and he entered the employment of the Tory Sir William Lowther, Second Earl of Lonsdale, who held political beliefs at odds with his own. It is a drama about the conflict between an art that reached for the profound and the pedestrian stuff of home life. As if, for him, they presented an inherent dichotomy.

In the interval, I step outside and walk down to the lake edge. The sun has set, and the sky is washed out peach fading into murky blue, behind charcoal mountains and islets, trees like a ripped sheet of paper. A single star has risen above a low band of cloud. It's generally a little unfashionable now, to think of the arts in such terms, as something striving to the transcendent, an arrow pointing skywards, away from the earth. The preference is for arts that are grounded, political, pushing for change. But it's clear to me, now, why Wordsworth felt closer to the infinite here, why he stretched his hand to the things beyond earthly reach.

Later, I bump into someone I vaguely know in the foyer — there's that disorientating, dreamlike moment of recognising a face out of context, and then we both laugh and embrace. My acquaintance is here with the director of the play and invites me to join them for the last night party with the repertory company. In a hospitality room upstairs somewhere I get drunk on cheap red wine served in plastic cups, make friends with the cast and get into arguments about Brexit and the general election, property prices and gentrification. Outside the window, night glazes the water.

I feel, for a few minutes, like I'm part of this band; a bond has been forged by our distance from home, lifted up on the transience of the encounter. The party winds down and we walk back through the slumbering town, bathed now in sickly orange streetlights, laughing and chattering — our voices too loud in the empty streets. We part ways with arrangements to meet each other at the lake in the morning to swim, high on the promise of new friendship. I reflect, briefly, when I'm back in my bed, on the slippery overlapping communities that form in theatres, circles within circles — but then I'm fast asleep before I can finish the thought.

I stay overnight in a perfectly English B&B. In my single room beneath the eaves, there are shortbread biscuits, tiny sachets of UHT milk and an unfeasibly soft bed from which I find it hard to rouse myself in the morning. Downstairs, a fry-up is served on white-clothed tables in the dining room. It turns out that most of the other guests were at the theatre last night too. We exchange notes on the show over our bacon and grilled mushrooms. The set was extraordinary, we agree, and the acting was wonderful — it was just a shame the story of Wordsworth's sister, Dorothy, was sidelined. The conversation unfolds, the way it does in B&Bs over breakfast. I tell them about my book and before I know it they're all chipping in to make suggestions, the theatres they love best — Frank Matcham's Grand Opera House, Belfast; The Bush in west London; The Oldham Coliseum — sharing anecdotes of evenings spent in each of them, everyone jostling to explain why their proposed theatre is more deserving of being on this list than any other. They're all right, of course.

After breakfast, I return to my room and put my swimsuit on beneath my jeans and sweater, hide the B&B towel in my bag, and walk back through the snoozy Sunday morning to the edge of the lake. But my new friends message me; they're too hungover, they have to get into town, they've bailed. The little kinship of the night has disbanded, shifted off into its constituent orbits. I doubt I'll ever see them again, I think, as

I clamber in across weed-covered rocks.

I kick away from the beach, relishing the sting of the water, the view of mountains. 'A lake carries you into recesses of feeling otherwise impenetrable,' Wordsworth wrote. Perhaps, after all, gaining on nature through art isn't about stretching away from our own sphere, but a means instead of sneaking up on ourselves. Those golden daffodils of Wordsworth's aren't lovely for their own sake but for the way they shape thought, enable him to slew off his 'pensive mood'. He asked his readers really to look at, really to see, the natural environment they inhabit, and by so doing to attain a deeper connection with themselves.

As I swim further out, I roll on to my back, and look towards the shore. In the distance, I can just make the theatre out: the discreet wall of glass at the front of the café, and the chevron of the roof, pointing up above the trees.

18

TOM THUMB THEATRE

Margate, Kent

Bingo halls. Jim Davidson. A glass of urine. Queen Elizabeth II. Tomato ketchup. Dirty Bitch.

I ARRIVE IN MARGATE on a winter's evening, long after the sun has set. I skirt the bay, passing boarded-up shops and a brightly lit yet desolate arcade, where a chorus of games consoles bleeps and hums and cuddly toys gaze out despondently from behind the glass of grabber machines. In endless rows of Victorian houses well past their glory days, bay windows are lit up, stages for miniature dramas: a woman in a dressing gown arguing with her husband over a bottle of wine; a pair of arms operating a weight machine; three men discussing a light fixture; someone slumped in a corner, head in hands. There are banks of hotels untouched since the 1970s, their lobbies ablaze and empty. Outside the Margate Winter Gardens, posters advertise gigs by Jim Davidson and Psychic Sally.

Overshadowing the beach is the silver crate of the Turner Contemporary. The painter J.M.W. Turner was one of Margate's most celebrated enthusiasts, and the gallery is situated on the site where he stayed, in the home of his mistress Sophia Caroline Booth. Opened in 2011, the Turner was the hallmark project in a multimillion-pound enterprise to regenerate this neglected seaside resort. Soon afterwards, Mary Portas, the acutely bobbed poster girl for noughties pop-up proprietors, began a scheme to revive the high street. Dreamland, Margate's iconic amusement park, was reopened, repackaged for a culturally savvy new day tripper.

Amid the closed down Primark and Peacocks concessions,

there are signs that this regeneration is taking hold: tiny hipster bars and shops with geometric idents, purveyors of craft beer and Danish furniture. Now Margate is commonly referred to as Shoreditch-on-Sea, which seems to me rather a faint compliment, but no doubt is music to the ears of anyone in the north Kent property industry. In 2015, house prices in Margate grew faster than anywhere in the country.

The philosophy of regeneration might be read as the philosophy of Peter Brook's *The Empty Space* writ large, in that it views a town as a palimpsest on which a new narrative can be written, rather than a locale with established identities at risk of being displaced. The disparity between the entrenched character of the town and what's superseding it is plain to see in the juxtaposition of bingo halls and quirky handicraft stores.

Academics have looked critically at the arts-led regeneration of Margate. 'It might become a very cool place to be, a very middle-class place to be, but is that really solving the problem of entrenched poverty and social exclusion in the town?' asked Jonathan Ward in a 2016 interview with *The Guardian*, following the publication of his research in this area.

From the outside, the Tom Thumb Theatre looks unprepossessing: a converted garage, flush to the road, gloss red frontage smudged with exhaust from the cars that thunder past. An incongruous balcony with an ornate balustrade circles the first floor; it looks like it's been borrowed from an Alpine ski lodge. A row of posters advertises forthcoming shows, an eclectic mix of performance art, cinema and jazz.

A man in a tweed coat is struggling to get in the door. I smile politely at him, and (perhaps this is ungracious) test it myself — it is, indeed, unyielding. Then we spot a narrow fire escape staircase, trimmed with fairy lights, running up to the first floor. Inside is a ramshackle cocktail bar, squeezed into what was evidently once the front room of a residential flat above the garage. The walls are painted burgundy, and a bar in the corner has been crafted from wooden panels. A turret window overlooks the street, lined with a spider's web of cracks, panes rattling with traffic.

The patrons are a mixed crowd, many alone, congregated on mismatched furniture around an ineffectual convector heater. They sit about wrapped in their winter clothes, sipping cocktails, reading books, engaging in small talk, clouding the air with their breath. The scene is presided over by a portrait of a youthful Queen Elizabeth II, who looks like she's having a grand time.

The Tom Thumb is 'one of the smallest theatres in the world', a chocolate box space that boasts an enviable league of fans.

My friend who recommended it wrote, 'It's a 39-seater red velvet intimate venue on the seafront run by a really nice couple who programme whatever they like and serve cocktails in the room upstairs.' This strikes me as a very fine policy for running a theatre.

It was here long before Margate got cool again. The theatre was built as a coach house in the 1890s, then in 1984 was transformed into the theatre, drawing much of its original clientele from the Butlins resort just over the road. The first owner was 'very eccentric'. Apparently, in the early days there was no bar but audience members would be issued with a thimble of sherry on arrival. The curious moral code of the proprietor was such that she banned cross-dressing in the pantomime. During performances she would sit on a stool at the back of the auditorium, ensuring no one was talking.

In the bar, I meet the current director of the theatre, Jessica Jordan-Wrench. She tells me that when the original owner died in 2009, the theatre went up for auction, and there was a discussion about it being turned back into a garage or housing. So her family decided to club together to buy it.

"My cousin had saved money to buy a flat. My aunt talked her into buying a theatre instead." I point out that running a theatre isn't an entirely typical family pastime — what about hiking or playing Scrabble? — and she shrugs. "It was really cheap."

Jordan-Wrench and her partner, Eoin Furbank, a theatre technician, moved down from London to run the venue in 2012. They converted the flat upstairs into this cocktail lounge. With no budget they made do with whatever they could lay their hands on, building the bar from parts of an old shed, decorating it with odd strips of wallpaper. Their first venture was to stage a twisted Christmas cabaret with their own theatre company, .dash, in which Jordan-Wrench herself played a "suicidal mermaid". It ran for five weeks. Few people came. "It was a baptism of fire, but it was also hilarious," she says.

Over time, they have developed an audience. There is no great agenda. The programming manifesto is simple: "It can be any form and it doesn't have to be easy, just that we feel from an audience perspective it's going to be interesting." A typical week might feature a film night, an experimental work of performance art, a bluegrass gig. The mixed bill is a way of encouraging people to try something new, the rationale being that if they come for something they know they'll like and have a good time, they might be persuaded to come back for something else. "The film nights are like the gateway drug, we get people in and tell them about all the theatre shows," Jordan-Wrench explains.

We're interrupted, often, as she greets the people who wander in. The guy in the tweed coat she says she recognises and asks him if he's been before. He was here a year ago, and they fall into conversation about the show he saw. I ask one of their regulars what keeps him coming back. "It's the people of course," he says, and they chuckle.

I think about the regeneration happening in Margate and wonder where the Tom Thumb Theatre sits in relation to that. The truth is complicated to unpick. The theatre undoubtedly contributes to the hipster cache of the town, as Talking Heads on the stereo and Swamp Donkey and Dirty Bitch cocktails on the chalkboard menu attest. It seems to me as significant that the couple doesn't earn their living from the theatre. "It washes its own face, but we have day jobs." Jordan-Wrench has worked as a journalist, an arts producer, a musician, a youth support worker. Their production assistant, who joined as an intern, is the only one getting paid. The artists who perform are unlikely to make much on box office either. The work presented here is done so principally as an act as grace.

This attitude extends to how the team deals with audiences. "We try and be just really lovely. It's not only about saying 'we are welcoming to everybody' but it's actually welcoming them, and if somebody does need a helping hand over the threshold then giving them that. There was a woman who had never been to the theatre before, and she came to see Sink the Pink — a 'world famous genderfuck army' — on her 60th Birthday. She loved it," Jordan-Wrench says, with a grin.

"It's really communal, because it's really small, people get chatting. We've had people who have lived on the same street for a decade and never spoken to each other, and the first time they speak is here."

I want to talk to Jordan-Wrench about this more — about what is required to welcome a community. But it's getting busy, and she has to jump behind the bar, and it seems obvious that of course everything would be much better if directors of theatres spent much less time answering hypothetical questions about who they're making work for and more time behind the bars of their theatres talking to them instead.

Then, it's 7.30 p.m. and time for the show to start — we tramp back out into the night, clutching our beers and our Amaretto Sours, and head down into the theatre. Behind the lacquered garage doors, in a small room beneath a low ceiling, faded tip-up cinema seating is arranged in a shallow rake in front of a tiny stage, framed with red velvet curtains. The piano in the corner has seen better days and the walls are decorated with burgundy and gold flock wallpaper.

Jordan-Wrench has expressed a cynicism about the trappings of traditional theatres ("I think as soon as you walk into a theatre, there is a kind of perceived behaviour, a feeling about how you should behave"), yet in many ways the Tom Thumb Theatre calls on the romance of the traditional auditorium. It's seductive, this stuff — and maybe theatre folk find it difficult to let go of all that beguiled them in the first place. Or maybe this is a form of reclamation, of subversion.

The performance tonight is an eccentric one-woman show mixing autobiography with a discussion of the ethics of working-class labour in modern Britain, peppered with bad but enjoyable renditions of *Bugsy Malone* songs and Tina Turner. At the Tom Thumb, the usual rules of theatre that require the audience to sit quietly and watch don't seem to apply. An audience member pipes up with a question about something she doesn't understand; someone else joins in with the chorus of 'Tomorrow', loudly. Halfway through the show a delivery boy turns up with 20 portions of chips that have been ordered in for us. They are passed around and we all club together for the tip, then tuck in, arguing over the ketchup with greasy fingers.

At one point, the artist on stage urinates into a glass and then drinks it. It is a reenactment of something she has genuinely done in her working life outside the theatre, accepting payment to do exactly this as part of the webcam work she's taken on to support herself. The moment is designed to shock. But the audience response is humane and intelligent; there is some laughter, and a couple of squeals, but glancing around I see that no one is covering their eyes, or making for the exit. They are meeting the artist's gaze.

In moments like this, I'm reminded of a film clip of John Cage, the avant-garde composer most famous for *4' 33"*, performing his experimental piece *Water Walk* on 1960s American popular reality TV show, *I've Got A Secret*. Presenter Gary Moore introduces Cage's performance (which to a general TV audience may have seemed deeply strange, with its orchestra of water pitchers, bathtubs and ice cubes) as follows, "he takes it seriously, I think it's interesting, if you are amused you may laugh, if you like it you may buy the recording."

As theatre-maker Andy Field has pointed out, it's a most gracious introduction to an artistic experience: an invitation 'simply to experience it, and even possibly to like it, without needing entirely to understand it' — a provocation to meet unfamiliar ideas and ways of being in a spirit of curiosity and with a willingness to respond honestly. At its best, this is a habit of engagement with the world that the arts encourages, and it is in the modest, generous places like the Tom Thumb Theatre that it seems most possible.

Is it ridiculous to look around a room full of smiling people looking at a woman drinking her own piss from a glass and feel hopeful?

The next morning, I wander through the town to Dreamland, past pastel signs with knowing slogans. *A thousand smiles an hour. We cater for pleasure.* The fairground is closed and the arcade mostly empty, save the roller disco. A bunch of children are squealing and tripping their way around beneath flashing lights, soundtracked by songs from *Frozen*.

Outside there's a carousel with the words *Young and Old Alike, Rode By All Ages* inscribed around the top in amaranth and cerulean cursive. The scenic wooden railway, which I'm unable to ride out of season but happy to admire from the ground, arcs overhead. The serpentine line it carves against the silvery winter sky is a thing of beauty.

Here is the Ferris wheel that has dominated Margate's skyline since 1980. Jordan-Wrench's theatre company, .dash, made *Passing Phase* here as part of the Margate Festival in September. A performance art spectacle in which each of the 24 carriages held a light, blinking out a word in Morse code — in unison, at first, but then beginning to fall out of sync. "It's about chaos theory, how everything is moving from order to chaos," she explained, "but that's OK, because that's how things are meant to be."

Jordan-Wrench and Furbank are giving up the Tom Thumb Theatre now. They have been careful to pass it on to people they believe will maintain the spirit of the theatre — another young couple. It feels like time to move on. They'll focus on the work of .dash, who have made shows in warehouses, galleries and clubs, but rarely in a conventional theatre. "I have nothing against theatres," she says, "but a lot of people do perceive theatre as not being for them."

The 2015 Warwick Commission report found that 'publicly funded arts are predominantly accessed by an unnecessarily narrow social, economic, ethnic and educated demographic not fully representative of the UK's population'. This fact is particularly pertinent in Margate, where the arts have been deployed as part of a deliberate plan to change the profile of the town. The Tom Thumb Theatre is set apart from this programme of arts-led regeneration; passion drives this enterprise, not money or political agenda. Besides, it was here long before the new wave of galleries and pop-ups. It is an established feature of the landscape. I can understand why, though, in this context, it would seem necessary to interrogate where you present your work, and who might therefore encounter it.

There was a moment in *Passing Phase*, Jordan-Wrench tells me, when she turned around and noticed a line of kids; they'd jumped the fence to get into the car park to skate, but were standing there, skateboards at their sides, just taking in the spectacle. And from the big block of flats nearby — all the way through the performance there were flashes in the windows as people took photographs with their phones. Their own messages, blinking back into the night.

Later, I email Jordan-Wrench, and ask her what the word

spelt out in Morse code by the lights on the Ferris Wheel was.
'HOPE,' she writes back.

19

NATIONAL THEATRE WALES

The size of Wales. An abandoned steelworks. A replica German village. The Manic Street Preachers. Bright House. A roll of stickers.

THE SIZE OF WALES: 20,779 square kilometres. Population: 3.063 million. Length of coastline: 1,400km. Unemployment rate: 5%. National languages: two. National parks: three. Mountains: 138. Median weekly income: £498. Take a map. Trace its border with your finger. The measure of icebergs, asteroids, depleted rainforests — it is precisely the size of a theatre. A national theatre without walls, the entire country as its backdrop; every member of the population a potential cast or audience member.

It may seem to stretch the scope of my journey to include a theatre without a single window or door to its name, but I cannot ignore the people who, when asked, nominated theatres that are not really theatres at all: caravans, stone circles, the palm of a hand. The provocation, I think, was to interrogate the bounds I'd imposed on my own project. I wanted to celebrate theatres, but it was also necessary to admit that — as Jordan-Wrench pointed out — "a lot of people perceive theatre as not being for them". If the artform broke the fourth wall long ago, it's impossible to ignore those who have gone further — who have smashed the brickwork and shaken the very foundations.

So here I am in Port Talbot, a modest town on the South Wales coast, a stone's throw from Swansea. I'm staying in a rundown hotel on Aberavon Bay, adjacent to a drive-through

Burger King and overlooking a crescent of damp sand. In the distance three cranes extend over the sea. Beyond them, a line of chimneys spews feathery smoke into a yellow sky. *If you can smell Sulphur in the air, it means someone in Port Talbot is getting paid.* For a brief time, in March 2016, these steelworks were at the top of the national media agenda. Looking out of my window, I try to remember their significance. There were mass redundancies, protests and picket lines, the story of an industrial town losing its industry and being left to disintegrate.

We're Still Here is the name of tonight's play. The roving spotlight of the news may have moved on swiftly from the events of that Spring, but the story wasn't concluded. Kully Thiarai, National Theatre of Wales' artistic director, tells me she was developing plans for a project in the Valleys with theatre company Commonwealth, co-creators of the show, when the *Save our Steel* campaign began — the movement opposing the changes at the steelworks. They were considering the question of where the working-class leaders are in modern society — suddenly, in Port Talbot, they had an answer. For 18 months, they have been working with the people of this town to create a new site-specific play exploring what happened in the wake of the redundancies and the threatened closure of the works, based on interviews with those involved.

"I call Port Talbot the shanty town. Because nothing

is right here." My taxi driver and I are lost in a tangle of backroads, looking for the old Byass Steelworks, where tonight's performance will happen. We end up down an alley, in a scatter of out-of-the-way factory buildings. I urge him to drive on through a set of gates into the overgrown carpark but he refuses. "It might be dangerous." Eventually we come across a man in high viz at a roundabout, looking remarkably upbeat in the torrential rain. He waves us in the right direction. The performance will indeed happen in an abandoned factory building in the middle of an overgrown estate; we just hadn't been at the right one.

At the entrance, I'm approached by a woman wielding a spool of *Save our Steel* stickers. She plants one on my anorak, then refreshes my memory on the background to the campaign. In March 2016, Tata Steel, the company that owns the local steelworks, announced the planned sale of its loss-making UK plants. A few weeks before, 750 Tata employees had been made redundant, in a town where there isn't an awful lot else to do. It looked likely the Port Talbot plant would close, leading to the direct loss of a further 4,000 jobs (including, she tells me, that of her husband, who had been employed at the steelworks for 37 years and was one year out from collecting his pension), and a wider impact on a community of people largely reliant on the plant for their livelihood.

Port Talbot — more often sped through on the M4 en

route to Swansea and the Pembrokeshire coast — suddenly became a staging ground for a major political battle. It was a year on from the General Election, a few months after the surprise choice of Jeremy Corbyn as leader of the Labour Party, and just before the referendum in which the UK (and Port Talbot voters) opted to leave the European Union. This neglected industrial town seemed to symbolise a struggle that was animating the politics of the moment — against the damage wrought by multinationals and the failure of the system to protect the interests of working-class communities.

The factory is huge: an expanse of concrete roofed with rain-thumped corrugated iron, disappearing into dry ice and low lighting. Buildings this large are only erected to contain industry and technology; perhaps religious rituals too, places of the expansive and marvellous. There's a tremendous sense of liberation in refuting the traditional theatre building, stepping out into spaces like this. "The freedom of not having our own building allows us to have a diversity of output — how we tell a story, where we tell it," Thiarai says.

Founded in 2009, NTW's 'theatre without walls' model follows an approach developed by National Theatre of Scotland and Theatr Genedlaethol Cymru (the Welsh language national theatre). In the wake of devolution in 1997, there was a demand for new national theatres to be established in Scotland and Wales. But the enterprise of building a new venue seemed too costly and complex; a national theatre fitted to the 21st century should be light on its feet, mobile and adaptable.

I have touched already on the potentially alienating power structures and associations implied by a theatre building. These problems become even more pronounced in the context of a national theatre. Where do you put it? What kind of work do you plan to accommodate there? How do you future-proof it — ensuring it will be fit for the evolving artform in decades to come? Denys Lasdun's brutalist National Theatre on the south bank of the Thames, for all I love it, is unwieldy, lethargic, destined to pursue the evolution of the form rather than to drive it. Calls have come to demolish it, or at least close it down for a while, forcing the organisation out of its box to explore the corners of the nation, rather than hunkering down in so many tonnes of concrete.

"There's a distaste that goes back centuries, relating to the history with England, to centralisation in any form," says John McGrath, founding artistic director of NTW. The obvious answer was to develop productions for touring, but this presented practical challenges, as Wales doesn't have a significant infrastructure of receiving houses suitable for large-scale productions.

A sense of place was crucial to the team's idea of what a national theatre should be. "Often theatre ignores place and pretends it's nowhere, but it is a unique group of people in that time who are only in that place once together, and so we can take the essence of theatre and make that how we explore 'nation' — what does it mean to be in this place and who is in this place," McGrath says. The model they decided on, in which productions would be developed in specific locations through focused periods of work *in situ*, borrowed both from the Welsh tradition of the national Eisteddfod, a roaming festival of music and culture that takes place in a different location each summer, and from the prevalence in the 1970s and 1980s of site specific theatre by companies such as Brith Gof.

National Theatre Wales launched in 2010 with 'a theatre map of Wales': 12 productions in 12 months, delineating not only the landscape of the country but also the possibilities of theatre in this nation. The first show, *A Good Night Out in the Valleys*, was mounted in miners' institutes across the South Wales Valleys. Soon after, an opera was staged in an abandoned library, a new version of Aeschylus's *The Persians* in a replica German village in the Breacon Beacons, built to train soldiers during the Cold War. "Sometimes we just shut down the Cardiff office and all went to live in Anglesey or Treorchy — everyone went on this adventure. It was not without its conflicts, because it's an intense way of asking people to live with each other. But out of those conflicts comes something different," McGrath tells me.

The last production of the year was presented here, in Port Talbot: a promenade retelling of the Passion of Christ that extended across the town over three days, created by and starring one of the area's favourite sons, Michael Sheen. It was an epic undertaking. In this town of 37,000 people, an estimated 1,000 joined the cast and a further 1,000 contributed in some way to the play's creation. Earlier, when I was hiding out in my hotel room, waiting for the rain to ease, I watched a BBC documentary about the making of the play. Based loosely on a secular reinterpretation of the Passion, instead of pursuing a rigid three-act structure, the play was amorphous, expanding to incorporate the creativity of the whole Port Talbot community. So the local rugby club became a security force, and an entire choreographic sequence was devised in response to the sounds and movements created by a young girl with profound and multiple learning difficulties. The creative team made it up as they went along, with whatever resources they could lay their hands on. At a special concert marking the Last Supper, local boys-made-good, *Britain's Got Talent* winner Paul Potts and the Manic Street Preachers performed. Up to 12,000 people witnessed the culmination of the play. Sheen was raised aloft on the crucifix on a roundabout right outside my hotel and recited memories of Port Talbot contributed by the people of the town. A remarkable event that touched the life of almost every Port Talbot resident, one way or another, and which laid out the stall of NTW perfectly.

We're Still Here begins. We follow the action as it weaves through piles of rubble sprouting dead flowers, steel towers and a flatbed truck that becomes a stage. The cast includes Port Talbot residents, recreating the picket line, union meetings — a splintered portrayal of what happened in this town, woven with earthy humour and a litany of expletives. Fragmented voices recount what it means to lose a job you take pride in, waking up every morning to an empty day ahead, how the hope leaches out of you. "Nobody listens. Nothing changes." The ghosts of the future haunt this spot; children, played by local teenagers, vanish out of sight, already lost.

The outcome of the protests was, in fact, broadly positive. Tata abandoned their plans to sell the steelworks and committed to millions of pounds of investment at Port Talbot. 4,000 jobs were saved, although the unions had to agree a cut to their members' pensions. The livelihoods of this community look relatively secure — for the time being, at least. In the end, *We're Still Here* is about how popular collective action can change the plot.

Afterwards I bump into the woman with the stickers and her husband. They're buzzing. "That was very emotional," he tells me. "That's exactly how it was! The conversation on the radios, everyone effing and blinding, I've heard that conversation a hundred times." They offer me a lift to my hotel, and in the car the woman tells me being involved with the project has reawakened her passion for theatre. "I remember going to the theatre with my mum when I was young. They stopped closing the curtains between scenes and she said 'it's not right! You can see everything they're doing!' So Lord knows what she would have made of this!"

The next morning, on my way to the station, I pass through the Aberafan shopping centre. It's a drab scene, with closed shop units and a few clusters of people milling about, clutching buckets of caffeinated milk from Costa. Here is a Bright House — one of those hire purchase shops with inconceivable interest rates that thrive in poor industrial towns. I recognise the shopping centre from the BBC documentary. Sheen's character, The Teacher, was reunited with his mother in the plaza after going missing for 40 days. Activists clustered on the escalators, protesting the arrival of a new road through the heart of the town — the local rugby team-cum-security squad restrained them.

Soon, the circus will be gone. The NTW banners will disappear; the cast members will be back at work. Thiarai acknowledges that the transient NTW model presents issues. "The difficulty is legacy," she says. "We can't return to every place in six months, so part of the work is empowering communities to continue the legacy."

For tonight, Port Talbot has reclaimed its own narrative. *We're Still Here*. That title works two ways. Not only as a reminder of those who get left behind when the camera lenses turn away, but also as an expression of resilience. "Over the last 18 months, we've been told ... this is what's happening to you, doom and gloom," cast member (and steel worker) Sam Coombes told Channel 4 News, who had returned to Port Talbot to report on the show's opening. "Well the true story is that we stood together and we fought."

20

CAMDEN PEOPLE'S THEATRE

London

*Henna tattoos. Two chintzy armchairs. Golden horns.
Onion bhajis. ANONHI. A hatstand nobody uses.*

IN EUSTON, EVERYTHING IS CHANGING. HS2 is coming. The future, exactly as it was foretold — bright tubes of expensive metal, shuttling people at 250 miles per hour to Birmingham and the North. Everything is getting faster, more efficient, more expensive. The Government's new railway line will take a slice out of the city, cutting north from Euston station into Camden, curving out over Regent's Park, west to Old Oak Common, then through the Chilterns, a £55 billion vein through housing estates and ancient woodland.

It is the future and it is already here, in the scaffolding going up around Euston and the roadworks churning up the concrete in the streets nearby. Outside St James' Gardens, a man in bright orange security overalls follows me as I take snaps of the tops of basketball nets behind new hoardings. In the summer a memorial service was held at the cemetery in these grounds for the 60,000 bodies that will be exhumed to make way for the railway, among them the former slave and celebrated boxer Bill 'The Black Terror' Richmond and Captain Matthew Flinders, the first man to circumnavigate Australia. How will he find his way back?

Drummond Street, though, is still redolent with spice, from its famous stretch of Bengali restaurants. I head west, passing the Diwana Bhel-Poori House and Ambala, purveyors of 'the finest Asian confectionary'. This community — like communities all along the route — is not giving way without a fight. Protests have taken place and representations made to Parliament select committees. 'STOP HS2' read the placards. 'NO BUSINESS CASE. NO ENVIRONMENTAL CASE. NO MONEY TO PAY FOR IT'. The imperative has gone unheeded. At what was once The Cottage Hotel, there is a sign demanding visitors 'STOP. PPE IS MANDATORY ON SITE'. The business has been subject to a compulsory purchase order in preparation for what will soon become the biggest construction site in Europe.

Camden People's Theatre clings to the corner of Drummond Street and Hampstead Road, in the midst of this shifting topography. My theatre — or at least, the theatre where I have been working since 2014. This is a homecoming, and also a goodbye. My tenure is reaching an end; the new year will carry me on to a new phase. Leave-taking imparts a certain perspicacity, and already I feel like I'm seeing the place from a distance. I romanticise this theatre, no doubt. I have loved it here.

I was 29 when I joined CPT as executive director, alongside Brian Logan, who has been artistic director since 2011. I was utterly naïve about how to run a theatre. I winged it with the help of Google and phone calls to better-informed acquaintances. What sustained me, more than anything, was my passion for the venue. I'd first come here in 2007 with a student production in my last year of drama school. What I found at CPT was kinship; it was scruffy and small, and yet stepping through the doors was a respite. Here, there was room to be yourself. The stranger, the better. Theatre-maker Nigel Barrett captured the venue perfectly when he said, in a 2014 *Guardian* interview, 'the first time I properly fell into the hands of the weirds was at CPT. It was 1995 and I auditioned for a physical theatre adaption of a Jewish short story. They said they gave me the job because they liked my jumper. I had been to drama school and done Howard Barker and Noel Coward.' Once you fell in, there was no way out.

The main body of the theatre is situated on the ground floor of what was The Lord Palmerston. Established in the 1860s, the pub was a vestige of the Victorian estate that once surrounded it. High up, from its grubby cream edifice, a late-flowering buddleia is sprouting. The building bears its history blatantly; the name of the Truman, Hanbury, Buxton & Co brewery is picked out in maroon lettering on the wall. On an illustrated panel adorning the façade, a man is mid-air kick, aloft in front of a full moon — a remnant of the building's days as the Yiahuang Martial Arts Centre, now faded blue by sunlight. Security signage warns that the building is protected. The theatre occupies the ground floor and basement; the three floors above are the territory of property guardians, those denizens of the city's liminal places. At an upstairs window, someone is either doing yoga or blowing their nose.

The foyer and office area are located in a dull, red-brick structure extending southwards from the old pub along Hampstead Road. The architecture of the building is itself a manifestation of the clash of wills that urban regeneration so often induces. This part was built in the wake of the so-called Battle for Tolmer Square, a 17-year struggle against the redevelopment of this area by property company Stock Conversion, who intended to clear the old Victorian housing and replace it with new office buildings. When plans became clear, squatters moved into derelict buildings, painting and repairing them, turning unused land into a makeshift playground, and even mounting the Tolmers Village Carnival, with a Punch and Judy show and a Guess How Many Peas in the Jar competition. The area became the 'locus classicus of London's intellectual squatting movement' according to Todd Longstaffe-Gowan's *The London Square: Gardens in the Midst of Town*.

In 1975, the BBC broadcast a documentary about the occupation which was heavily critical of Stock Conversion's plans; the redevelopment was subsequently cancelled. Instead, the site was purchased by the London Borough of Camden and turned into the mix of social housing, commercial and offices that stands here today. The Lord Palmerston closed in 1981, and since then the premises has had various guises, including as a community centre and martial arts centre. Camden People's Theatre has been here since 1994.

It is apt that this venue stands in an area synonymous with social struggle. CPT emerged directly from the Unity Theatre, a national 'volunteer' arts movement that began in the 1936 and was closely linked to the trade unions and the Communist Party. Based in a converted chapel just north of here on Goldington Street, the Unity Theatre staged performance of direct relevance to working-class people, including the premieres of plays by Bertolt Brecht and Sean O'Casey. The movement is credited with launching the careers of actors like Michael Gambon, Bob Hoskins and Warren Mitchell. Paul Robeson, the internationally renowned entertainer and civil rights activist, turned down West End work to appear in *Plant in the Sun*. "Joining Unity Theatre means identifying myself with the working class," he commented at the time.

These were pioneers of 'Living Newspapers' and agit prop. During a period in which mainstream theatre culture was dominated by light entertainment, the fare on offer at the Unity was radical. Take their show, *Babes in the Wood*, which satirised appeasement, and in particular Neville Chamberlain. A question was raised in the House of Commons; there was discussion of shutting the Unity Theatre down, but nothing came of it and the play was a smash hit. The author H.G. Wellls was apparently so taken with another performance,

Waiting for Lefty, that he leapt up on his chair, waving his umbrella around and joining in with the chanting: "Strike! Strike! Strike!"

When the Lord Chamberlain's censorship ended in 1968, mainstream theatres were able to stage more provocative and political content; the urgency of Unity Theatre's offer waned. Then, in 1975, the Goldington Street property burnt down. A note in the Unity Theatre archives at the Victoria and Albert Museum reads, 'It's gone now, burnt down, I think by fascist elements of the maniac Right. It may have been bad electrics, but who is to say?' Afterwards, the group spent years searching for a new base, considering numerous potential sites including Toynbee Hall, Wood Green Trade Union Centre, the Marx Memorial Library, the Albany Empire and the Round Chapel in Lower Clapton Road. Eventually, the council agreed to let them lease 58-60 Hampstead Road for one year. A letter from the Chair of the Unity Theatre Society reads, 'For the society to continue it needs a 'home' — without which then we might as well disband the organisation. Tolmers could hopefully provide a new beginning?' In 1993 they moved in.

But things were never the same and Unity Theatre's presence here was short-lived. Management committee minutes from the period demonstrate that tensions were simmering among the group running 58-60 Hampstead Road. On 14th February 1994, they record friction about a critical letter that had been sent by one of the group to another: 'S. wanted it to be recorded that she felt that B.'s letter was unacceptable. Others registered their view that it was acceptable. B. rejected remarks about his letter. T. objected to B.'s letter. C. stated that people should say what they felt; that was the purpose of socialist theatre!' When the lease came up for renewal, two members of the group decided to submit an independent bid for the site. The bid was successful, and Unity Theatre had to move out.

Sheridan Bramwell was the first artistic director of Camden People's Theatre. "She got loads of people involved," Lynne Kendrick, one of the founder members, tells me. "This was before social media so down at The Actors' Centre there'd be a sheet of paper — 'come and get involved, we're interested in new artists and new people'. It was a brilliantly naïve move. Because none of us really knew what we were doing. And we went 'oh great, that's a good idea — yes I'm not doing anything else this summer, let's go and paint this venue'."

CPT was situated in the heart of a racially divided community. In the first eight months of 1994, 117 racially motivated attacks in the area were reported to the police. Then, on 13th August, Richard Everitt, a white boy, was stabbed to death by a group of Asian teenagers in Somerstown. Everitt's murder inflamed tensions, and the media reported revenge attacks, 'gangs of white youths, sometimes 20-strong, roaming nearby neighbourhoods'. "I remember one evening we were working late and we opened the doors and looked up Hampstead Road and it was full of kids kicking the shit out of each other. So it was a very, very different area at that time, and there was a lot of anxiety," Kendrick says. In *Bengali Backlash*, a 1997 documentary that explored the lives of young Asian men living around Drummond Street, one teenager says, "I see Hampstead Road as a boundary line. On my side of Hampstead Road we feel safe, on the other side is Robert Street. We feel like we can't go there because we might get beaten up." Passing through the streets of the local area, the documentary captures how the young men are the subject of racial slurs in the street.

In this landscape, Bramwell emphasised socially engaged theatre, developing projects with local community groups like the Asian Youth Association and the Surma Centre. Ajay Chhabra, future star of *The Archers* and *The Basil Brush Show*, directed an ongoing project for the main stage called *Intercity Lives* with local teenagers.

CPT was also a home for more European modes of practice — collaborative, non-script-based work. "It was often stuff that was very risky, very marginalised," Kendrick tells me. "Because of the nature of the place I think it very much impacts on the nature of the programme." Many companies have passed through the doors over the years, including Fevered

Sleep, The Pacitti Company, Cartoon de Salvo, Ridiculusmus, Blind Summit, companies making innovative, radical work on the outer edges of the British theatre sector.

Today, the venue is dedicated to staging 'contemporary theatre by emerging artists about the issues that matter to people right now'. We've had festivals exploring the housing crisis, feminism, London's air pollution — a gamut of concerns the Unity Theatre team might have recognised. A few weeks ago, we threw a street party with the residents of Drummond Street. We ate onion bhajis, wrote funny poems and rapped with five-year-olds. The scene was not so different from the Tolmers' Village Carnival Day, all those years ago, except now instead of Morris dancers there were beatboxers, henna tattoos in place of face painting.

Inside the maroon double doors is a wood-panelled bar that doubles as the box office. Strings of festoons cast light on tiny tables with dog-eared William Morris print oil cloth coverings. Posters for forthcoming shows line the walls and a smeary blackboard is chalked up with *What's On*. In the window stands a miniature stage, two moth-eaten armchairs and a hatstand nobody ever uses.

"I can't walk in that theatre without feeling really emotional," Kendrick says. "Because the daringness of it, particularly in the early '90s, of setting up a space, and saying 'we're going to make theatre in this space' was lunacy, fucking lunacy to be honest, we could barely get it licensed let alone get anyone to come and see us... I'm in my 50s now but I was in my 20s when it was set up — we were all very young and naïve and you never get that again, I don't think I'll ever get it again, so I miss that."

Through another set of double doors is the theatre: a black box studio. In spite of the faithful, regular repaintings it receives — the technical manager staying late after shows close so it will be dry in time for the next day's get-in — it is always pock-marked and scuffed. 35 worn, blue seats in a rake; at the front, benches strewn with scatter cushions. The narrow strip of stage. The fire doors that open straight on to the noise and traffic of Hampstead Road. "If someone stands there having a fag outside the fire exit, that's it, your show is ruined," Kendrick says. "Or not — depending on how you see things. So completely not fit for purpose. This is what's brilliant about CPT. It's absolutely and utterly unfit for purpose in terms of the real business of making theatre, but that's what made it make great theatre."

Former artistic director Chris Goode wrote in *The Forest and The Field* of how, during his tenure, he came to see the noise from the street as a kind of 'litmus test' for the attitudes of visiting companies. 'There were those for whom it was, without question, a black mark against the venue, a failure to show proper respect for their work by protecting and insulating it from the crude and inevitable (but unpredictable) intrusions of the urban environment around us; and there were those who accepted it with patience and equanimity and perhaps a little curiosity as to what would be visited on them in the next performance and how, if at all, they would respond.'

Sometimes it seems there isn't much space in the city for places like this anymore, by which I mean to say, marginal places, places that are rough around the edges, places that don't easily fit the narrative of growth and progress. Statistics from the Mayor's office reveal that in recent years, more than 50% of London's night clubs and music venues have closed down — among the prominent casualties have been queer venues The Black Cap and Madame Jojo's. There are new cultural venues opening too, many of them shinier, better equipped and better appointed. This is what makes a city, isn't it? The only constant is change. Businesses close down and others open up where they stood. There can be a pigheaded sentimentality in clinging to buildings that are shoddy or unfit for purpose. It was ever thus.

Well then, I am sentimental. I'm sentimental about the grime rap battle, the artists who lived in our windows for three weeks. Because I think that we need these gritty places in the skin of the city. They become homes, sometimes, for gritty people too, people who disrupt complacency, forge alternative ways of inhabiting the urban space. A necessary grit from which great pearls may develop.

The foyer is full of the cast for tonight's show — the opener for our autumn season. The room is littered with their empty coffee cups and sandwich wrappers. On the stereo is a 'gender queer' playlist — Bowie and ANOHNI. One of the company jokes about how they watch *999: What's Your Emergency?* to relax after a day in rehearsals. "When you spend your life making art, you have to get some reality to chill out," they say, self-deprecatingly, and everyone laughs.

One day, I think, I'll come back, and this will be a branch of Costa. I'll sit here and drink my Frappuccino and remember the time two artists urinated on each other in that corner just there. Or: I'll come back and nothing will have changed. There will still be the broken lift and the leaking roof, that chintzy armchair in the window that someone reclaimed from a show, only that I'll be a stranger, the theatre too full of new energy to make room for my nostalgia. I feel on the cusp of it all, the way autumn's windfall seems to bring not loss, but new potential. I hope it falls into the possession of those that are more troublesome to the city than I could ever be. I bequeath them the entire fucking kingdom.

"It's lasted a hell of a lot longer than I thought it was going to," Kendrick says. "So that's something."

In the evening, the new season opens with *Bullish*, a take on the myth of the minotaur with a cast of trans and genderqueer performers. It's a show about how being neither one thing or another can beautiful, an exultant celebration of in-between lives, in-between places. There is glitter and music and golden horns, and the audience is ecstatic — wild and up on their feet.

After the performance we hang around drinking in the overcrowded bar. Everyone is high on having created something that really works. How easy it would have been not to; how easy not to do this at all. We all had a part to play in bringing this creature shuddering to life, and like the minotaur, it is a complex, fabulous beast. The world will be a little better for it. Later, we drift off up Camden High Street to a dive bar where one of the performers from the show is doing a drag king cabaret act. I buy everyone Jägerbombs and dance, badly and extravagantly.

Maybe this is what I've been striving for all along. This sense of belonging somewhere. This moment when everything is in order, when for a few moments you are not looking to the future, but thinking, I'm inhabiting this right now. It's happening right now. What do you with the 'terrifying revelation' of the present moment?

Theatre would have us live it, and let it go.

§

One of the best things we ever staged at Camden People's Theatre was a show called *O No!* by Jamie Wood. It was an irreverent theatrical homage to Yoko Ono, in which Wood created a series of avant-garde artworks, following the guidelines set out in Ono's *Grapefruit: A Book of Instructions and Drawings.*

Invited to join him in the realisation of one of the pieces, an audience member stepped on stage and climbed into a bag with him. Together, slowly, in the awkward space, avoiding the tangle of limbs, they took their clothes off. For a few minutes, they were naked together, and in the torch lit intimacy of the bag, they talked about human relationships. About love. Then, they put their clothes back on, and the show continued.

I think about that moment, often. I'm pretty certain that that audience member didn't walk into the theatre at the start of the night thinking, 'I'm going to get naked with Jamie Wood on stage tonight'. But somehow in the 40-odd minutes that elapsed in between, the mysterious chemistry of theatre worked on them. It may sound strange to say this of watching two people take their clothes off in a bag, but that moment made me hopeful about what theatre makes possible.

Hope. That's what this is all about, really. It is hope that has motivated me to come to work every day, to continue with the often unforgiving business of running a theatre, of stressing about whether anyone will show up and how we'll pay for it all, of dealing with funding applications, marketing campaigns and flooding toilets. And I suspect it was hope that motivated Rowena Cade, as she dragged her bags of sand up that cliff face; Dennis Neale, as he crafted a proscenium arch from a broken tea tray; Alan Lane with his pots of vegan stew; Jatinder Verma with his shower of yellow rose petals.

We need this more than ever, now. At its core, what we're witnessing around the world — as borders close down, migrant communities are maligned, and cultural differences quashed — is a struggle over what it means to be together in the same place. In this context, a theatre is a symbol and an expression of an idea: that being with other people is better than being alone. That coming together to engage with different views and ways of living in the world is not only necessary — it enriches us. It is much harder to ignore the plight or destroy the life chances of a person whose gaze you have held. Sharing space is the beginning of kindness.

I don't think the version of theatre I'm describing always reflects the theatre as I currently experience it. But on this journey I have seen glimmers in the dark. The reason I value that moment in Wood's show so greatly is because I believe it was the the collective goodwill of the people in that place, on that night, that was able to uphold a gesture that in most circumstances would seem deeply strange, and yet was somehow transformed into something not only natural, but inevitable. What else might we achieve together, if we put our minds to it?

To recognise this power in theatre is not to suggest that things are good enough as they stand. The writer Rebecca Solnit says that hope suggests that 'another world might be possible, not promised, not guaranteed. Hope calls for action; action is not possible without hope.'

So read this as a provocation: to seek out a theatre that is more true to its essence than ever before. In this model of a democratic space — how is difference represented? Whose voices are heard? What does difference mean? How do we meet and hold one another's gaze? What makes us hopeful?

If we can find our answer in a theatre, we might find we understand our world a little better too.

THANKS

I would never have made this journey, or written this book, without all the encouragement and inspiration I have received. Particularly I would like to thank Tom Chivers and James Trevelyan at Penned in the Margins for believing in the book from the beginning and nurturing it so kindly. Thank you to the Society of Authors for supporting me with the Michael Meyer Award.

I have been overwhelmed by the generosity of all those that I have met at theatres along the way. Zoe Curnow, Simon Goldrick, Steve Tompkins, Deborah Aydon, David Jubb, Bethany Haynes, Nina Dunne, Verity Leigh, Sam Gough, Dennis Neale, Barrie Hesketh, Philippa Comber, Alasdair McCrone, Alex Stevens, Jatinder Verma, Matt Fenton, John McGrath, Alan Lane, Lucy Hind, John Beasley, Patric Gilchrist, Conrad Lynch, Jessica Jordan-Wrench, Kully Thiarai, Lynne Kendrick, and all the very many others — thank you.

I have some brilliant friends who have always been there for me: Dan, faithful fellow wild swimmer; Honour, hardy fellow ghost hunter. Laura Barnett has been a constant source of wisdom and support, and Dan Richards picked me up at a difficult time. Lydia, Maddy and Goo, thank you for always being at the end of the phone or ready with a thoughtful message or 'care package' exactly when I needed it.

My colleagues at Camden People's Theatre were a model of patience when I decided to take off on this hare-brained adventure. Brian, Anna, Kate and all the board — thank you for giving me the space and support to make it happen. The chapter on Contact contains some text that previously appeared in a blog post written for *The Stage* — my gratitude to them.

Those who have shared your pearls of wisdom on intriguing, remarkable theatres I would never have discovered otherwise — you are too many to name, but I couldn't have done it without you.

Thank you to my amazing mum and dad for always believing in me. And to my kind, beautiful aunt Ros Pearce, who was very much loved and is very much missed. This book is for you.

SUPPORTERS

To my generous crowdfunders: I thank you heartily.

Katharine Turner, Anthony Villis, Bush Moukazel, Roma and Geoff, Sally Rose, Susie Safavi, Lydia Evans, Eve Leigh, Megan Vaughan, Luke Wright, Billy Barrett, Rob Palk, Nicki Hainey, Jo and Chris MacDonald, Dave Smith, Olly Hawes, Kate Cross, David Ralfe, Barrie Shapiro, Goo & Gaia Reed-Birks, Raz Shaw, Trisha Waters, Caroline McGuffie, Becca Pratt, Nicholas Cassen, Daniel King, Tom Stevens, Ann Clark, Tania Harrison, Susan Kempster, Cressida Brown, Thea Platts-Mills, Barbara E Workman, Gavin Barlow, Luke Evans, Flavia Fraser-Cannon, Eleanor Turney, Andy Field, Jamie McLaren, Aurelie Gouaux, Patrick Birley, Anisha Fields, Emma Stenning, Gemma Goggin, Theo Bosanquet, Stella Duffy, Jon Gilchrist, Ruby Glaskin, Alex Thorpe, Tom Wicker, Tyler Wetherall, Kate Thorogood, Sally Homer, Sam Dunham, Matt Trueman, Kirstin Shirling, Sarah Wilson-White, David Arnold, Henry Hitchings, Jonathan Wakeham, Alex Eisenberg, Megan Bommarito, Roland Smith, Jonathan Harper, Leanne Glover, John Osborne, Chris Brett Bailey, Anna Fessenden, Andrew Zadel, Anothny Gray, Melinda Haunton, Miriam Gould, Adam El Hagar, Agatha Yerbury, Tassos Stevens, Sam D Grover, Julie and Phil Thompson, Paul Burns, Effie Loy, Laura Barnett, Dan Richards, the Bealeys, Maddy Mills, Talia Kelly and Valerie Foster.

The boost was not only financial; your vote of confidence made me believe that I could do it, and spurred me on when the going got tough.

Austin, JL, *How to Do Things with Words* (Harvard University Press, 1975)

Batty, Michael, *The New Science of Cities* (The MIT Press, 2013)

Berger, John, *Here is Where We Meet* (Bloomsbury, 2006)

Berger, John, *The Shape of a Pocket* (Bloomsbury, 2002)

Brook, Peter, *The Empty Space* (Penguin Classics, 2008)

Billingham, Peter, *Theatre of Conscience 1939-53: A Study of Four Touring British Community Theatres* (Routledge, 2001)

Carlson, Marvin, *Places of Performance* (Cornell University Press, 1993)

Carr, Lydia, *Tessa Verney Wheeler* (Oxford University Press, 2012)

Correri, Augusto, *In Place of A Show* (Methuen Drama, 2017)

Derrida, Jacques, *Deconstruction is/in America* (New York University Press, 1994)

Dyer, Geoff, *White Sands* (Pantheon Books, 2016)

Earl, John, *British Theatres and Music Halls* (Shire Publications, 2005)

Gallagher, Lyn, *The Grand Opera House, Belfast* (Bliackstaff Press, 1995)

Goode, Chris, *The Forest and The Field* (Oberon Books, 2014)

Hankinson, Alan, *The Blue Box, The Story of the Century Theatre 1947-1983* (Bookcase, 2009)

Hesketh, Barrie, *Taking Off: The Story of the Mull Little Theatre*

(The New Iona Press, 1997)

Hess, Scott, *William Wordsworth and the Ecology of Authorship* (University of Virginia Press, 2012)

Hill, Leslie & Parris, Helen, *Performance and Place* (Palgrave Macmillan, 2008)

Leacroft, Richard and Helen, *Theatre and Playhouse: an illustrated survey of theatre building from ancient Greece to the present day* (Methuen, 1984)

Lerner, Ben, *The Hatred of Poetry* (Fitzcarraldo Editions, 2016)

Levin, Bernard, *The Pendulum Years* (Hodder & Stoughton, 1989)

Longstaffe-Gowan, Todd, *The London Square: Gardens in the Midst of Town* (Yale University Press, 2012)

Morrison, Lucy and Stone, Staci L., *A Mary Shelley Encyclopedia* (Greenwood Publishing Group, 2003)

Orgell, Stephen, *The Illusion of Power: Political Theater in the English Renaissance* (University of California Press, 1975)

Phelan, Peggy, *Mourning Sex* (Routledge, 1997)

Reid, Trish, *Theatre & Scotland* (Macmillan, 2012)

Rolleston, Maud, *Talks with Lady Shelley* (Folcroft Library Editions, 1925)

Rufford, Julie, *Theatre & Architecture* (Palgrave Macmillan, 2015)

Sachs, Edwin, *Modern Opera Houses and Theatres* (ReInk Books, 2015)

Sinclair, Ian, *London Overground* (Hamish Hamilton, 2015)

Trelawny, James, *Recollections of the Last Days of Shelley and Byron* (Da Capo Press, 2000)

Vitruvius Pollio, Marcus, *Vitruvius. The Ten Books on Architecture,* translated by Morris Hicky Morgan (Harvard University Press, 1914)

Ward, David, *encore! Ten Years of Theatre by the Lake* (Bookcase, 2009)

Wates, Nick, *The Battle for Tolmers Square* (Routledge, 2012)

Wheeler, Mortimer, *Still Digging* (Pan Books Ltd, 1958)

Wilmore, David (ed.), *Frank Matcham & Co* (Theatresearch, 2008)